D1484417

Carry On
and
Ditch the Excess
Baggage!

A Journey through
Depression, Divorce & Cancer

Tiffany Allen

ISBN: 978-0-9979227-0-7

For Mop(py), Dad(dy),
Jer, Bre, & Troy—
I'm everything I am
because you loved me

TABLE OF CONTENTS

Introduction 7

Chapter 1: Insecurities Abound 11

Chapter 2: Embarrassing Moments................ 18

Chapter 3: Life is Precious 27

Chapter 4: A Ray of Light.................................. 37

Chapter 5: A Prior Engagement 47

Chapter 6: Southwest & Swedish Fish............52

Chapter 7: Sinatra Says it All 56

Chapter 8: From Cracks to Chasms.................59

Chapter 9: Wild Animal..................................... 73

Chapter 10: Desperate Times 78

Chapter 11: Surfer Ken......................................84

Chapter 12: Don't Deny the Denial 88

Chapter 13: Sentimental Stuff 93

Chapter 14: I Don't Do Pink.............................100

Chapter 15: Don't Want to Miss Anything 109

Chapter 16: Humor & Needles....................... 113

Chapter 17: Roses & Thorns............................ 126

Chapter 18: Owning My Ugly............................129

Chapter 19: Who am I Writing For? 140

Chapter 20: The Ancient Shrink & Pale Girl 146

Chapter 21: Mental Meltdown.........................154

Chapter 22: Smelling Frosting 165

Chapter 23: Soberanes..............................172

Chapter 24: Sonya..................................179

Chapter 25: Eggs & Firemen.........................183

Chapter 26: Please Validate Me!....................190

Chapter 27: Happiness Project & Hypnotist 198

Chapter 28: Mama Bunny & Map Theory.....202

Chapter 29: Hard & Sailor 207

Chapter 30: Three-Pronged Forgiveness......213

Chapter 31: Let It Be 219

Chapter 32: Changing Perceptions 222

Conclusion...227

Editor Outtakes.....................................230

Acknowledgements 234

About the Author....................................237

Introduction

Dear bad luck, let's break up.—Unknown

I read a statistic once that breast cancer survivors are 8% less likely to divorce. So maybe if I had just waited to do the marriage thing until after the breast cancer, I might have had better luck staying married. But I'm not typically known for having the best luck.

My questionable luck with men started at an early age and at a place known for creating a mood for love, at least for a three-hour session—the roller skating rink. I was at the fourth-grade skate party and Bobby Lukes was the essence of cool. He had a turned up collar and a perpetual sneer. When he asked me to skate, I was so grateful for the hours I'd spent learning to skate backward. As we took our awkward turns around the disco ball lit rink, love blossomed. The next day, he called me and said he wanted to ask me a question. He then spelled out the entire phrase "Will you go with me?" one letter at a time, as I pretended with each letter that I had no idea what he was getting at.

I covered the phone and asked permission from my mom who was sitting nearby, working on one of her many sewing projects. Before she said okay, she wanted to know just what "going with a boy" meant. I told her it just meant you told people you were going together and you hung out together at recess and lunch.

"Do you hold hands?" she asked.

"Eew, no!" I said, although deep down, I had a secret desire to know what Bobby's hands felt like. With Mom's permission, Bobby and I were "going" with each other. I couldn't imagine anything separating us. After all, this was a committed relationship.

One day during recess, Bobby's friend Carlos told me he needed to talk to me. I can still picture the exact location of the chain-link playground fence where Carlos and I stood.

"Bobby wants to break up with you," Carlos said.

"What?!" I was shocked. "Why?" I stammered. There was no way I could have foreseen what came next.

"Because you're not allowed to say fart."

I was speechless. I was crushed. But then my rising anger took over and I marched over to Bobby and said, "Fart, fart, fart, fart, fart!" Not my classiest moment, but I felt confident that he was appropriately shamed. This was just the beginning of many loves gone wrong and my tale of survival.

After Bobby, there was Dean, the boy who lived behind me. I thought Dean was the love of my life. We even had a song, "Almost Paradise," from the movie Footloose. It *was* almost paradise until he moved away in the 7th grade and later went to jail for grand theft auto. However, Bobby and Dean both paled in comparison to Jason, the most popular guy in high school. When he offered to be my first kiss, I was sure I had died and gone to teenage heaven. Just one month later, when he broke up with me at a party and then went back inside to high-five his new girlfriend, I began to doubt that Prince Charming really did exist.

But my faith was restored by Tyler, the cutest boy in our apartment complex in college, the one all the girls liked. He was the epitome of tall, dark, and handsome. When he said he wanted to marry me, I'm pretty sure time stopped. But this time, my insecurities got the better of me and any faith in myself sunk like the proverbial lead balloon. I was sure there was no way someone that perfect could stick with someone like me long-term. I sabotaged any chance of a future with him.

But long before Bobby, and long after Tyler, there was always B. Our parents were close friends, and he was a couple of years older than me. He was the one on the pedestal, the completely untouchable one, the one who made my 4-yr-old heart actually flip inside my chest if he smiled. He could also crush me in an instant as was evident when I went to church wearing a new dress lovingly sewn by my mom with Strawberry Shortcake fabric. He and his friend made fun of it, and my mom was furious when after the long hours it took her, I refused to wear it again. But none of that stopped me from dreaming about a future with B. That's why one fateful day in 2005 (a mere 27 years into my harbored crush), upon learning that my parents would be attending his youngest sister's wedding reception, I threw out a last-ditch Hail Mary to my mom. "I'll give you a hundred bucks if you can get B to call me." Never had one off-handed comment changed the course of a life so drastically.

Chapter 1:
Insecurities Abound

The reason we struggle with insecurity is because we compare our behind-the-scenes with everyone else's highlight reel.—**Steve Furtick**

I grew up with an inferiority complex. If I wasn't feeling inferior to my best friend Natalie (a tall, dark-haired, statuesque beauty), I was feeling it toward my younger sister. Cute, popular and athletic, she seemed to have it all. She would eventually learn the hard way that popularity and talent came with a price, as she was picked on by the jealous girls and targeted by some she considered her closest friends. But to me, who didn't bring enough attention to my peers to even raise an eyebrow, I thought her life didn't look bad at all. I would've traded "mean girls" to be in the homecoming court any day! I was always taught that we were each unique with our own gifts, but that was hard to swallow as I stood in her wedding reception receiving line in an unfortunate "buttercup" yellow dress and had some well-wisher say to me, "Wow, it must be so hard to be her sister. She's SO beautiful!" My beautiful sister was 19 years old and marrying someone who my mom had warned me "looks just like Tyler!" Of course he did. I'd expect no less. I was 24 with not a prospect in sight. And yellow has never been my color.

My rock bottom self-esteem might make more sense if I had grown up in a highly dysfunctional home. I say "highly" because I've come to believe that all families have some degree of dysfunction. While my family was among the higher functioning dysfunctional families, no kid comes out unscathed. As the oldest child and especially as a girl, I took on the responsibility for many grown-up things that were not my problem or within my ability to fix, but I was sure that if I were a good enough kid, it would relieve some of my parents' stress, seemingly brought on by these grown-up problems they faced.

My mom would later say I was the sun and the rest of the family were the planets, but that wasn't obvious to me as a child. What was obvious was that I got tummy aches before anything stressful whether good or bad. Because this internal distress was no respecter of stress-type, my mom called it my "birthday party stomach." I would often curl up on the bathroom floor in a towel after my shower in the morning and just wait for my tummy to ease up enough to allow me to get ready for school.

I was plagued with horrible recurring nightmares that always started the same way. A giant bear standing on his hind legs would appear in my bedroom doorway. I could hear his raspy breathing as he stood there. Then he would eventually lumber over to my bedside and stand over me as I tried desperately to pretend I was asleep. He would then pick me up out of my bed and carry me to whatever bad dream was on the docket for that night. Sometimes I was rescuing my family from danger. Sometimes I was playing in a sandbox where hands would come out of the sand and pull me under. Sometimes there would be a city of miniature people living under my bed. I loved things in miniature, so I always hoped this one would be a fun dream where I could play with the little people in their little town. But they were always mean little people who would bite me. These dreams created all kinds of fears. I was afraid of trees, dogs, and rocking chairs. I still can't sleep in a room with a rocking chair. Mine used to come alive and rock by itself before it would attack and wrap its arms around me. Stephen King would be proud, right?

Birthday party stomach also affected my schooling. Because I did well in my classes, they tested me for the honors program in third grade. I failed the test. Each year for the next three years they would test me again and again. I dreaded it. Sometimes they would have me retake it in a classroom all by myself. Those were the worst. I failed every time. I was an A student who never made it into the honors program. I hated that test.

Like most kids, I really wanted to be liked. But I was not the most socially adept child. For my eighth birthday, I got to have a party. I was so excited, and of course so sick to my stomach. Before the party started I was trying to think of something "cool" for my friends to do when they got there. The only thing that came to mind was to tear pieces of party streamers and write my guests' names on them. Then I taped them to the wall so they could find their names when they first walked in. There were probably no more than six or seven people at the party, and when my friends got there I realized how dumb my idea seemed. No one ever said anything, but I was sure they thought I was a complete dork. That memory, like many other socially awkward moments, haunts me still.

Like a chick becomes a chicken, I grew from a neurotic child into a completely stressed-out, depressed teen who couldn't seem to find one good thing to like about herself. The worst part was that, in my awkward frustration, I turned to sarcasm. Not the funny/witty kind of sarcasm, but the mean/biting kind. I was sure that cynicism would make me look cool. Besides that, wielding this tough persona made me feel untouchable and less vulnerable. Like a child who covers her eyes believing that no one can see her, I thought this ruse effectively hid how desperate I was to be popular.

Don was one of the casualties of this sarcasm. My friends and I used to attend weekly dances in high school during which I always seemed to keep one eye on Don. He, on the other hand, wouldn't even acknowledge my existence. It seemed only appropriate to finally put him in his place. One night I marched boldly over to his group of friends and asked if he wanted to dance. After his flippant "I guess" response, I retorted, "Well I don't," turned on my heels and walked away. I thought that move was so cool for several years until I finally realized it was me who looked silly.

I started seeing a counselor my first year of college and basically haven't stopped since. I've had more counselors than I can count on both hands, and I've taken pretty much every antidepressant and anti-anxiety medication known to man. I just wanted to feel happy. I wanted to feel that little lift that comes when something good happens and you feel it in your chest. But all I ever felt was either basic survival, something below that bar, or just an overarching state of numbness.

After college graduation, I tried to fill the void with travel. My first big adventure was to visit my cousins in London, with a mid-trip jaunt by myself over to Paris. I was so proud of myself for searching online and choosing my own Parisian hotel, and I was prepped and ready for my first passport stamp. London was amazing, and as I headed off to Paris alone, I felt completely liberated! I was brave! I was tough! I could travel internationally all by myself!

I found my hotel and headed for the Louvre. I had only 3 days there and I had to make the most of it. I wanted to practice the four years of French I'd taken, but I hadn't a clue what most people were saying, and Parisians have zero tolerance for people "trying" to speak French. The funny part is, they also have little tolerance for people who speak English! It felt like a lose-lose situation. On day two, I had a run-in with a very mean lady at a perfume shop next to my hotel, and it ended with me in tears. The morning of day three seemed impossible to face. I called my mom from the hotel room and just cried. I don't remember what she said. I just remember I was eventually able to get up and get going. What she probably wanted to say was "Stop your crying! Do you have any idea how much I'd love to be in Paris right now?" But I was the sun, and she must have acted accordingly. That trip led to many others, and I found that I felt remarkably empowered when I was traveling. I did cruises, tour groups, humanitarian trips, and some that were just figured out as I went along. But the thought of coming home to my life each time was so overwhelmingly difficult that I sometimes wondered if it was worth going on the trip at all. How could I still be so depressed and unhappy with who I was? Would I always feel this way? What was my problem?

Chapter 2:
Embarrassing Moments

Whoever is in charge of making sure I don't do stupid things, you're fired!—**Unknown**

It became apparent in my early years that despite my neurosis and dark depression, I always seemed to end up in predicaments that made people laugh. After years of feeling laughed at, I finally started to realize that if I was laughing too, then I was being laughed with, and that seemed a whole lot more palatable. Sometimes making that shift was easier said than done, particularly because more often than not, these occurrences were quite embarrassing.

These embarrassing moments started early and left an indelible impression on my young mind. Flash back with me to sixth grade, when my two blonde best friends and I all liked Chad. Imagine my dismay when Chad decided that my two friends were both going to be his girlfriends. I never understood why if you could have two girlfriends, you couldn't have three. So I did what any heartbroken sixth-grade girl would do in this situation. I wrote Chad an anonymous note. One day we were both sent to the office to pick up something. I seized the opportunity and gave Chad my note that "someone" had asked me to give to him. He read it while we walked and then said matter-of-factly, "You wrote this." I tried my best to lie gracefully. He just laughed. I never admitted the truth. Needless to say, Chad left a mark. Not until our 20th high school reunion was I able to even speak of it to him. Thankfully one of the blondies was there to corroborate my story since Chad had no memory of the "best two out of three" incident. Selective memory, I'm sure. I was also a little surprised that he didn't still have the note. Doesn't everyone keep that stuff? I have plastic bins full of every note and letter I've received since the dawn of time. Well, since third grade to be exact. If I had received that note, I would be able to retrieve it in seconds, as it would be conveniently bundled this very moment in its plastic bin home, filed by sender. Is that weird?

My embarrassing moments continued and included things like shooting at the opposing team's basket at a high school basketball game against our biggest rival (I was a horrible shot, so thankfully I missed). They also involved me leaving the lunch table one day in high school to come back and find someone had taken my Big Hunk candy bar. I gave everyone grief trying to weed out the culprit. No one confessed. Math class was next and I was asked to do a problem on the chalkboard. You know how when you write on a chalkboard, sometimes your behind jiggles a little? Well, I figured the giggles from the class were because I must have had an extra jiggle that day. I tried to stiffen up but to no avail. The snickers were just fueling my annoyance that had begun with the stolen Big Hunk. Fast forward one more class period and my friend Skye and I were walking home from school. She stopped to tie her shoe and I kept walking. Suddenly I heard an exploding laugh from behind me and I turned to find Skye hunched over, almost rolling in the dirt. Holding her stomach with one hand, she pointed the other toward me. "I FOUND YOUR BIG HUNK!" As luck would have it, the missing Big Hunk was stuck to the back of my shorts. "Big Hunk Butt" became one of the many "terms of endearment" I would inherit over the years.

There was also the time when the aforementioned high school dreamboat Jason and his best friend thought it would be funny to lock me in the glass display case outside one of the classrooms right before the final bell rang. I had no choice but to strike a pose and hope I blended in . . . to a computer-aided drafting display.

I briefly mentioned shooting at the wrong basket but truly, high school basketball was a hotbed of embarrassment. One day I had another friend who came running up to my lunch table with the same spasms of laughter that plagued my friend Skye during the Big Hunk incident. Again there was the holding of the stomach and the pointing of the finger. This time, the finger was directed at the compound where my book locker was. "YOUR LOCKER'S ON FIRE!" he finally belted out. What?! I ran over to find one of the security people pulling the charred remnants of my books and my basketball practice bag out of my burning locker. To this day, I still have no idea who set fire to my locker, but what I do know is that I wore Converse hi-tops for the rest of my basketball career that had "Converse" melted down the back of them. "Flamer" became another term of endearment. I'll admit that I did find a little satisfaction when my coach asked why I wasn't wearing my red shirt for practice that day and I was able to legitimately tell him, "My locker got set on fire and my shirt burned up."

Because we allowed the opposing team to use the girls' locker room during half-time, basketball also provided a rare opportunity to visit the boys' locker room for our own half-time talks. Rather than sit on the floor with most of my teammates, I would always sit in the back of the room on the sink to hear whatever lecture was coming from our coach. During one half-time, when my coach was in a particularly foul mood and yelling quite loudly, I suddenly heard a loud crack and felt myself falling. I crashed to the ground in a pile of shattered porcelain and water. That pretty much killed any seriousness in the room. Oddly enough, the very same Don from dance rejection fame complained to me the next day about how the boys' locker room was closed off "because some idiot broke the sink off of the wall." I chose to remain anonymous.

In grad school, on my way home from class one afternoon, I got into an accident and totaled my first car, a little Nissan Sentra. I had a terrible itch on my foot and was trying to remove my sandal with the other foot in order to scratch it. The freeway traffic came to a sudden crawl and

I tried to veer off to the shoulder to avoid hitting the car in front of me. The problem was the car in front of me had the same idea. I tried to find the brake with a sandal dangling from my foot but could only manage to find the clutch. I hit the car and knocked him down the shoulder. Still unable to find the brake and still traveling faster than him, I actually hit him a second time. When we got out of our cars to exchange information, he looked legitimately scared. He apparently figured with two hits, someone must be coming for him. As we exchanged information, he sucked the life out of several cigarettes and said he didn't want to call the police. That was fine with me. He would later sue me for pain and suffering due to his inability to play pool. Go figure. As it turned out, my totaled car was still drivable. I got $3k from the insurance and bought my car back for the salvage value of $700. As a business major, I thought it was a pretty smart financial move, but I was mocked incessantly about that car. My MBA classmates thought it hysterical that I would arrive at job interviews in my ten-year-old beat up Sentra with no front bumper. That may be why I never got any local job offers. Instead, I ended up in Huntington Beach, California.

One night, exactly one month after moving to Huntington Beach, there was a fire in the adjacent apartment. Apparently my roommates and I were all heavy sleepers because the firemen ended up kicking our door in, and I awoke from my air mattress (too cheap to buy a bed) to a 6'7" fireman standing over me. It was one of my finer waking moments for sure. After getting us up and out of the apartment, the four of us single gals were able to hang with some of the firemen out by the fire truck. Eventually, we even got them to agree to a picture with us. As this was prior to the digital age, it wasn't until I got my pictures developed that I realized my roommates had chosen not to tell me that I still had the big white dots of toothpaste all over my face that I had applied before bedtime to clear my acne.

One of the highlights of my embarrassment reel happened when I was working at a Food Bank after college. I thought it would be nice to take Dy, our new employee, to lunch. I wasn't feeling too well that day, and my stomach was pretty rumbly, but I thought a lunch out would help her feel welcomed. As we drove in her car I realized my gastrointestinal tract was in bad shape, so I tried to carefully let out the gas bubble that seemed to need release. I suddenly realized it was far more than a gas bubble. Thankfully we were next door to where my dad worked, so I jumped out of the car as she waited in the drive-thru line and told her I was going to say hi to my dad and I'd be right back. I ran straight to the office complex bathroom, stripped down and surveyed the damage. I could get most of the evidence out of my khaki pants but my underwear was completely ruined. No problem. I figured I'd just ask Dy if we could stop at the Walgreens next door so I could "run in and grab something." My restroom delay meant Dy ended up paying for lunch but thankfully she still graciously agreed to my request for another stop. It wasn't until I was getting out of the car at Walgreens that I realized I had completely forgotten my wallet. I was busted. I sheepishly explained what had happened and asked her if she could float me a loan to buy myself a pair of underwear. Thankfully Dy had a great sense of humor; however, she insisted that if she was paying, she got to pick them out. Forever after until their dying days, those Garfield underwear always made me think of Dy.

The list could continue, but I'll spare you any more details. I tell these stories for a couple of reasons. First, they give a little insight into the girl with the low self-esteem who just couldn't find her cool factor or any cool factor for that matter. Second, because I survived them. The upside of survival is that you typically come out of it with a few lessons learned. In my case, surviving is still a work in progress; therefore, my story is one of lessons still being learned. I call them "Lessons Learning."

Chapter 3:
Life is Precious

Sometimes even to live is an act of courage.
—Seneca

After my broken engagement to Tyler and another broken engagement to a boy named Justin shortly after college graduation (name changed because I still deeply care about this person and want to minimize any potential for hurt), I started to feel like maybe there wasn't a lasting relationship out there for me. I went the next two years through grad school and then five years living in Huntington Beach without going on a single date. Southern California was particularly rough for me. I called it "the land of the pretty people," and I was completely out of my element. I found an apartment with three other girls that I was pretty excited about, and I was super pumped when they called and told me they had talked it over and wanted me to move in. I would be sharing a room with the one girl I hadn't met yet. Sherri. I walked into my new room as she was getting ready for one of the many dates I would watch her go on while we shared living space. She had long blonde hair (unbeknownst to me, she was a natural brunette) and was tall, slender, and beautiful!

Sherri was from Kansas. She had moved to California to escape small town living and try her luck in the big city. Immediately intimidated by both her beauty and kindness, I began my downward spiral in the land of the pretty people. I would be reminded over the course of time though that, like my little sister, not all pretty people had it perfect. Sherri was my biggest lesson.

Sherri was not only beautiful and kind, she was generous and unselfish. She was spiritual and humble. She was strong and vulnerable. She lived her life just looking for ways to do things for other people. She would spend half an hour before bedtime in prayer and religious studies. Not having been taught solid financial principles, she looked for guidance from others and whittled her way out of significant debt. She was likable and sweet. She became my dear friend.

When I bought my first house in Huntington Beach, a two-bedroom condo within two miles of the coast, Sherri eventually moved in and became my roommate again for a period of time. It was during this time that I realized my pretty friend was struggling. Just as I had for so many years, Sherri battled depression and a huge feeling of inadequacy. She believed that if she could just be a good enough person she would feel better. So no one, and I mean no one tried harder than Sherri. She would comfort a friend until all hours of the night while still making sure to get prayer time in before falling asleep. She would drive anywhere (in her car which should have been given last rites a decade earlier) to help a friend, and she would get involved in every way she could think of to serve a stranger. She was truly one of the most loving and tortured souls I have ever met.

After Sherri moved out of my condo, she began dating Zach. She wanted more than anything to be a wife and a mom and Zach was good to her. She adored him. But her depression just wouldn't let up. Lacking insurance, she was unable to get help and unable to move forward with Zach because she just wasn't sure it was "right." After all, she still felt sad.

One night I came home from work to find Sherri's car parked in my one-car garage. I was quite annoyed since she didn't live there anymore. I went inside and could hear that she was in the shower. I knocked on the bathroom door and called her name. No answer. I knocked and called again. Eventually, the door cracked open and I could see that she had stepped out of the shower covered in soap from head to toe. She told me to go look in her car. Still irritated, I went to the garage and grabbed the single sheet of paper I saw on her passenger seat. It was a letter to God, an apology for not being able to handle things anymore. She had planned to sit in my garage with her car running and end her life. For whatever reason, she couldn't follow through and was now just sitting in the shower in tears. I went back upstairs and told her to get dressed and come out. I took her to a crisis center where the police were called. Later when I came back to pick her up, she seemed fine. She was embarrassed that the police had been involved and that a big fuss had been made over the whole thing. I was both relieved and angry. I was scared not only for Sherri but also for me. I had already come incredibly close to making that same decision myself, and watching this happen brought back a lot of fear and memories. There had been a time when ending my life seemed the only hope for relief.

I had moved to Huntington Beach to take a job that would train me to be a nursing home administrator. I thought it a little crazy that the company would let a young twenty-something run such a complex organization, but the craziest part was that I was their first master's degree hire. Thus far all the others had only held bachelor's degrees. I was already worried that their expectations of me would be too high to achieve, but I really liked the idea of taking struggling organizations and turning them around, which was the modus operandi for this start-up.

I trained for a year and a half under a wonderful mentor and friend and hoped that at some point, I might be able to run the flagship building where I had learned the ropes. I was passionate about what I was doing and noticed that for the first time since I could remember, I didn't have stomachaches in the mornings. I actually got out of bed looking forward to going to work. I was eager to get there and see what the day would bring. I felt safe. I felt purposeful.

But isn't it sometimes the case that we throw ourselves at one thing to avoid our inadequacies at something else? That is exactly what I did. I worked long hours at that building because I was too afraid to try and have a life in Huntington Beach. The land of the pretty people was completely intimidating. If I worked sixteen-hour days though, I didn't have to feel guilty about not having a life. That became my life.

After a year and a half, I was given the chance to run my own building. I got a call one night that a change in leadership was being made at a facility just 3 miles from where I was training and that I was to be there at 8 a.m. the next morning. That first day, I had just a few hours of overlap with my predecessor and then he left for his next assignment. When he walked out the door, he took the air from my lungs with him. I completely fell apart. I don't think I fully comprehended how severe a panic attack could be until that moment. I literally couldn't function. I couldn't leave my office. I was paralyzed with fear. I called my mentor at the building down the road and he came and got me. I couldn't stop crying. I felt there was no way I could ever go back. But I knew that I had no other choice but to return, despite the fact that I literally believed that if I walked back into that building I would die of fear.

But I walked back into that building for a year and a half. It was the darkest period of my life up to that point. After each night of restless sleep, I would wake sometime between 3 a.m. and 4 a.m. I kept my phone by my bed so that as soon as my eyes opened I could just grab it and call my mom. When she answered the phone I rarely spoke. I would already be sobbing with fear and dread. She would talk to me for upwards of a couple of hours until I could drag myself out of bed and into the shower. I would then meet my mentor at his building, my safe place, and he would talk to me until I could get myself to go to my facility. Once there, I would put on my best act and try to be a leader. But inside I literally felt that I was dying. I really believed this fear would kill me. But I also knew that if I ever let myself not show up one day, I would never show up again. I followed this morning routine for at least three months until I could finally at least get myself to work without the two-hour call to mom and a visit with my mentor.

Lesson Learning: Fear will not kill you. When you feel your ship sinking, hold onto loving family and friends as your lifeline.

Even after being able to get myself to work, I was a shell. I would put on my act for my employees but I would come home and have nothing left. My roommates finally pulled away, not knowing how to help and not wanting to be dragged into the abyss that seemed to surround me. I couldn't even form sentences to have a conversation with them. I really didn't believe a human being could survive this way for any length of time. I was dying. I knew it. The life had been sucked out of me as the door closed behind my predecessor and no matter how many times I kept showing up, it wasn't coming back.

I had never understood suicide until that point. I didn't necessarily want to die but I knew I couldn't live. I would drive to work on the freeway each morning and have thoughts like "If I just hit that cement barrier hard enough, I wouldn't feel anything. I'd be free. This unrelenting insurmountable pain would be gone." I had heard that sitting in your closed garage with your car running would allow the carbon monoxide to just put you to sleep without ever waking up. I wanted that. I wanted that so badly I could hardly stand it. I needed relief. My dreams were nightmares. My days were nightmares. There was no escape. I knew that my death would devastate my parents though, so I was trapped. There was no way out. I couldn't even kill myself.

But I needed the pain to end. I needed the fear and panic and dread to end. There was nothing that could save me and I prayed that God would take me in some natural way so the decision didn't have to be mine. He never did. Thankfully, my mom was always on the other end of the phone. She didn't let it leave her side for those 18 months. She was there during every early morning call, every middle of the night call, every desperate "I can't do this anymore" call. My mom saved my life. Years later, I found myself wishing I could have been that person for Sherri. We always question what more we could have done when we realize the degree of pain a loved one has endured.

The day after Memorial Day 2007, I was at work when I received an email. Sherri had passed away the day before.

After the near suicide at my house, my dear friend had eloped to Vegas with Zach. They had been married for a year. She was able to get on medication that helped her depression and allowed her to live a higher quality of life. She had always wanted to be a wife and mom, so when she got pregnant and heard that antidepressants could hurt the baby, she stopped taking them. Seven months into her pregnancy, her husband came home and heard the car running in the garage. Sherri had taken her life and the life of their unborn baby.

Sherri's funeral was packed with people. She was beloved by so many and each of us was dealing with our own devastation that we had not been able to save her. Doctors delivered Sherri's baby so that her husband could see his son. Most unforgettable was her viewing, where they had tucked her baby boy in her arm. Even years later I still have random moments when I think about Sherri. I believe in an afterlife and I believe that her spirit and that of her baby still exist. I sometimes wonder what they're doing, if she felt the relief that she so desperately sought, if the God of my understanding was a merciful God who welcomed her home. Life is precious, as are the friends and relatives who make up your lifeline. Sherri taught me that.

Chapter 4:
A Ray of Light

I want to be the reason you look down at your phone and smile. Then walk into a pole.
—Unknown

After barely surviving for 18 months as a nursing home administrator at that first facility, I begged for relief. A position was created for me that allowed me to travel to the other nursing homes and help other administrators. I loved it! I loved not being in charge but being helpful. I loved traveling. I loved hotels and airplanes and airports and solitude. Every week felt like some kind of adventure, and though I got a little tired of only being home for a couple of days a week to wash the same 5 outfits and repack them, I knew I could do this job forever. I was finally settling into a routine of sorts and, as I told my mentor at one point, I loved being the wind beneath the wings of other administrators. I was able to meet so many people from the company and I believed in what we were trying to achieve. I felt life coming back into me.

But I hadn't been on a date in seven years, and although I was fine being single, it was hard to not wonder what was so wrong with me. Instead of spending a lot of time ruminating about it, I just threw myself into work. Then came the fateful $100 offer to my mom.

Shortly after she attended B's little sister's wedding, I got a phone call from her while I was in Hawaii with my little brother. I knew she had told B's parents at the wedding about my offer to get B to call me, but I certainly didn't think anything would come of it. As it turned out, a lot came of it. When my mom called, she was almost panicked. B's mom had left a message saying that she had told B about my offer and, seeing as he had just gone through a breakup and thought the offer was pretty funny, he wanted my number so he could help my mom get her money.

Even as a little girl, B's mom always seemed to have a soft spot for me. When I was 11, she told my parents she would like to teach me piano. Since we didn't have the money to pay for lessons, she offered a payment option. I would make a dessert and bring it once a month to pay for my lessons. Although I didn't necessarily value piano lessons at that point, I loved getting to be around B's mom, and I loved any glimpse I got of B. I would get so nervous when he would occasionally burst into the room to grab something and run back out to play with his friends. I was sure this was what love felt like. My crush was not lost on B's mom, so I thought it odd that when my mom called to play me the voice message, it started with "Um, I'm not sure if it's a good idea or not but B wants Tiffany's number." How could it be anything but a good idea?!

"What do I do?" my mom asked.

"Huh? YOU GIVE IT TO HER!" Sheesh. I wasn't going to let this opportunity slip away like I had before. That's a story in itself.

Sometime after moving home following college graduation in the late '90s, my parents had received an invite to B's other sister's wedding. There was no way I was letting them go without me! I think I had seen B one other time since his family moved when I was twelve. I was not going to miss this. The whole evening was nerve-racking and I spent most of it trying to figure out what I could say to him. Finally toward the end of the night, when my chance was almost gone forever, I finally had it figured out. I walked up to him as boldly as I could and said, "Hey, have you seen my parents?"

"No." End of conversation. I went home a disappointed girl.

But many years had passed since then. It was May 2005 and thankfully, I had left some of that schoolgirl angst in the prior century. I was in a Texas hotel room when he called. I missed the call but when I saw the number I somehow knew it was him. He left the happiest voicemail I think I'd ever heard. Just the sound of his voice made me smile! It was the sound of the happy-go-lucky kid who had grown into a happy-go-lucky man, and I couldn't believe this was happening. I called back and got his voicemail. I tried to make my message sound as happy as his. Then I waited.

Truthfully, I had no thoughts of this going anywhere. Although we had both been raised in Mormon households, I had always planned on marrying someone with whom I could have a wedding ceremony in a Mormon temple. But I knew that after high school, he had stopped going to church and not only had little involvement with it but also was living a lifestyle that wasn't exactly conducive to the one I had envisioned in a partner. Looking back, that probably took the pressure off for me and allowed me to not be a total idiot when we talked. But despite having no expectations of us having a future at that point, I still wanted to be sure I came across as calm, cool, and collected and not like the star-struck little kid who couldn't form a sentence. Or even worse, the star-struck adult who could only muster, "Hey, have you seen my parents?" I had no intentions at all but still wanted to be sure I left a lasting (positive!) impression this time.

When he called back, we talked for what must have been an hour. I was shocked at how comfortable and fun it was. But I was also relieved. I had pulled off an intelligent conversation with my childhood crush! I definitely did not want him to call back . . . ever. I wanted him to be left with the memory of me being at the top of my game. Plus I was sure there was no way I could sound that normal for another whole conversation. But after a few days, he did call back. Our conversations went on for hours. They were nonstop. He was smart, funny, intellectual, and sweet. The conversations got more flirtatious. How in the world could this be happening? This was B for crying out loud! B, whom I had adored before I knew how to write my own name! B, who had once invited me to play Monopoly when we were at his family's for dinner. I was eight. He burned a hole through the Get Out of Jail Free card that night while "Private Eyes" by Hall & Oates played on his boom box. Memories like these were etched in my mind. And now he was flirting with me!

After a month or so of conversations, he informed me that he was coming to Huntington Beach for the weekend to see me. I was still in Texas during the week and he lived in Monterey, CA, about a six-hour drive from Huntington Beach. It was sometime in early July, and he said he would pick me up from the airport when I returned from Texas. I told him no way! Seeing each other would just wreck everything. I knew now that I could keep my cool on the phone with him, but there was no way I could see him. Out of the question! But as I would come to learn, when B got an idea in his head, that was just the way it was going to be. It's partly what I fell in love with.

He showed up in a red and white checkered shirt. He was smiling and still so cute, although somewhat older than the young man I remembered. We spent time together that weekend, and somewhere near the letter "N" while playing the country game, he kissed me. B . . . kissed . . . me! Given that our lives had taken somewhat different paths though, I still didn't see the possibility of us ever coming together. I shared that with him, and he seemed undeterred. He even started going to church again. He made changes in his life. He explained his decision to quit the baseball league he had worked hard to create because they played on Sundays by simply saying with his huge dimply grin, "I'm coming to play for your team."

I couldn't believe what was happening. I was falling in love. The first time he told me he loved me, I had backed him into a corner to get him to say it. After all, a girl's gotta do what a girl's gotta do! And I remember exactly when I knew that I loved him. He was supposed to come spend another weekend with me in Huntington Beach following my return from work in Texas. Facing a crisis at my job there, I called him completely distraught on the Tuesday before, telling him I wasn't going to make it home and how horrible everything was. By Thursday, he was in McAllen, Texas (he would never tell me what that plane ticket from Monterey cost). He was there to rescue me. I couldn't hold back. I told him I loved him. And boy did I mean it! He did everything he could to be helpful that weekend. He did awful manual labor at the facility, he listened as I vented about everything that was going wrong, and he comforted me. I still couldn't believe this was real.

We continued with our long-distance relationship. It was difficult for sure, but so amazing. I felt loved, beautiful, smart, and valued. I got care packages and sweet notes. I surprised him one weekend by driving to Monterey without him knowing. I still remember him saying he went completely weak in the knees when he saw me, but the best part was that as I threw my arms around him, I could actually feel him shaking. It was the most attractive thing ever! He was such a light in my life, and all I wanted to do was talk to him and be with him.

But I also continued to be tormented by those unrelenting insecurities, which led me to struggle with the relationship and doubt that it could ever go to the next level. I was worried about his commitment to religion, whether I loved him "enough," and whether my decisions were "right." I had always believed that before making a decision as impactful as marriage, you prayed and received some kind of "spiritual confirmation." Confirmation, I learned, is defined in a myriad of ways. When he started talking about marriage and how great it would be, I wasn't sure I could do it. I wasn't sure I could be a good wife. I wasn't sure I was "supposed" to marry him. I wasn't sure of much of anything. But there was one thing I felt sure of. I felt sure that he loved me. He loved me in spite of me. I felt safe in the knowledge that he would love me forever.

That one sure thing became the basis of my confirmation and gave me the ability to move forward with wedding plans. After several discussions about whether or not it was okay to get an engagement ring, I finally felt like I could do it. I could wear a ring on my finger. I could do the marriage thing. We would do it together. He would hold my hand through it. I wish I could say that was the end of my worry, but I was still plagued by the constant nagging of self-doubt and insecurity. Somehow in spite of those feelings, however, I felt safe. I felt that he knew the challenges that came along with my difficult package and he was ready to take them on. He was my eternal optimist! Nothing could discourage him.

Lesson Learning: Don't depend on others for your happiness. It's a completely inside job.

The thing I hoped for more than anything else was that through our relationship, I would learn to be more like him. I was the practical one, the disciplined one, the rigid one, the worrier, the planner, and the saver. He had a joie de vivre that was palpable. And he loved me. He truly loved me. I believed it with all my heart. By marrying him, I believed that what he had would rub off on me. How could I still suffer from depression and anxiety when I was adored and when I had a partner to walk the scary roads with me? I felt an unconditional love from him that made moving forward toward marriage seem possible. Given my history of two broken engagements, that was a pretty big deal.

Chapter 5:
A Prior Engagement

Good decisions come from experience. Experience comes from bad decisions.—Unknown

Starting high school is a bit nerve-racking for anyone, but this neurotic kid was particularly nervous. High school also meant attending an early morning religion class before school known as "seminary." It started at 6:10 a.m. It's not the ideal time for any teenager to retain anything of substance so I had a lot of respect for those who taught us (during my senior year that happened to be my dad).

During the first day of seminary, I recognized a kid I had seen at summer band camp. Justin had a big smile and was quite cute. He seemed pretty happy for 6 a.m., and he seemed to take a liking to me. He patiently stood on the sidelines as I swooned over the aforementioned Jason, but by our junior year, Jason had graduated and broken my heart. Justin was there to pick up the pieces. He had always been there. I was just too distracted to care. But we had become friends and I had spent time with his family, a blended family that totaled 15 kids at the time and would eventually add 4 more. I loved being a part of that family, and although I didn't feel as taken with Justin as he seemed to be with me, I was appreciative of the attention and validation. Justin took me to both my junior and senior proms. Junior prom was awkward but by senior prom, my feelings for him had matured. It was one of my best high school memories.

When I left the next year to attend college out of state, he moved to a town a couple of hours away to be close to me. But I wanted the college experience of meeting new people, dating, and hopefully falling in love. Justin was both persistent and willing to stand back and wait in the wings while I had my college fun. Two years after high school graduation, he left on a 2-year-long church mission. During that time, Tyler came along. Justin had become just a friend to me, an old high school boyfriend. I was a big college girl now, and Tyler was the man of my dreams. But even though Tyler seemed to love me, I just couldn't let go of the insecurities. They whispered that he didn't really know me and that if he figured me out, he'd turn tail and run. His gorgeous ex-girlfriend lived in the complex behind us, and I knew there was no way he could stay with someone like me after being with someone like her. Eventually, my fear of him leaving me became a self-fulfilling prophecy. It was slightly messier than that but that's a story for another time.

After college graduation, I moved back home to Phoenix. Justin was still there and we started to spend time together again. We had such a solid friendship that a serious relationship seemed like the appropriate next step. In the middle of the woods near his family's cabin, down on one knee, he proposed to me with a ring in hand. I accepted. But as we drove home, an uneasy feeling settled in the pit of my stomach. I stared out the window and wondered why I felt this way. Since we were fourteen years old Justin was sure he would marry me. My engagement to Tyler had only slightly dissuaded him. If he was so sure, then maybe I could follow his lead. He was my best friend after all, and don't you hear that great marriages are forged by marrying your best friend? So why did I feel so hollow?

Despite the fact that my parents were away celebrating their anniversary, this news seemed too important to sit on until the morning, so we crashed their party that night to show off my new bling. My dad even shared that he had written in his journal at some point years before that he thought I would marry Justin. Why was I not feeling that same certainty?

By the next morning, I was in full-blown gastrointestinal distress. I called in sick to work and then called my parents at their hotel to tell them I was on my way there. I was a complete disaster. I was sobbing and inconsolable. Oddly the person I wanted to console me was Justin and when he found out I wasn't at work and tracked me down at the hotel, I was both nervous and relieved to see him. If anyone could help me feel better, I knew he could. His words were sweet, kind and reassuring. I told myself I could do this. I think mainly I didn't want to lose him. He had been a part of my entire teens and now twenties. I couldn't remember much about my life without him. I didn't want to lose my best friend.

Lesson Learning: If your feelings aren't engaging, maybe you shouldn't be engaged.

I wore the ring for a month. During that month, I couldn't seem to find interest in looking at wedding dresses and I was never ready to talk about setting a date. I literally didn't want to plan a single thing. I couldn't take even the smallest step forward.

That's how I knew things were different with B. Despite my insecurities and fears, I could pick a date (which happened to be just 6 weeks after he proposed.) I could shop for a dress. I could take steps forward. I wasn't frozen. That was my confirmation. Plus I knew I felt differently when B got down on one knee. I knew he would protect me, love me, and keep me safe and I believed he could do it. I was as happy as my little, pained psyche had ever allowed me to be.

Chapter 6:
Southwest & Swedish Fish

Go for someone who is not only proud to have you but will take every risk just to keep you.
—**Unknown**

One of my favorite qualities about B was his creativity. His proposal is a perfect example. As I was on a flight with a coworker traveling home from work, I was a little caught off guard when the flight attendant came by with her bags of peanuts but also had a bag of red Swedish fish candies in her sack. B and I had an inside joke about red Swedish fish so I thought that was oddly coincidental. I had been flying every week for 3 years at this point so I was completely over the peanuts. I still can hardly even look at a peanut (unless it's covered in chocolate of course). Anyway, the flight attendant asked if I wanted peanuts and I said, "No thanks, but I'll take those Swedish fish!"

"Sure!" she said and handed them over. Weird.

Lesson Learning: Don't settle for peanuts when you can have red Swedish fish.

Truth be told, I had caught a glimpse of a flight itinerary in B's email and wondered if he might be up to something. I didn't know the details, and I had watched to see if he got on the plane and never saw him, but when the Swedish fish came I was on high alert. Something was happening. I remember telling my coworker, "I think B might be on this plane." But I looked and looked and couldn't see him. So I ate my red Swedish fish.

A few minutes later there was someone up front on the PA system. I usually tuned them out since I knew the routine. I even knew most of the jokes the Southwest flight attendants would tell. I vaguely remember that the voice started off by saying "Thank you for flying Southwest Airlines." But then something was different. The voice was describing a relationship. The voice was a voice I recognized. The voice was B!

I'm still not sure how he pulled it off considering this was post 9-11 and he was in the front of the plane near the cockpit. He later told me that's why he started with "Thank you for flying Southwest Airlines." He didn't want any of the passengers to think he was a hijacker and go all vigilante on him. I was impressed.

After some of the most beautiful things a girl could hear, I heard this: "I'm here today to ask her to marry me." Ever the window seat junkie, I had to clamber over my coworker and practically ran down the aisle. The passengers were going crazy with cheers. When I got to the front, he was down on his knee. The "yes" that came out of my mouth felt good this time. I was going to marry B!

I later learned that he had arrived at the airport super early and told the gate agents what he wanted to do. The wonderful people of Southwest will always hold a special place in my heart for the way they helped him. One astute gate agent even called B's cell phone at one point to let him know that he might want to rethink his plan since I was sitting, chatting and laughing with another guy (my coworker). She apparently didn't want him to set himself up for failure. One of the crew sat in the front row to hold a seat for him while everyone boarded and then they somehow made a human shield to get him on board without me noticing. Some of the passengers near him even wondered aloud if he were a celebrity.

The plan was for the flight attendant with the Swedish fish to offer me peanuts and when I said no (which B knew I would), she was supposed to say, "How about some red Swedish fish?" Well, leave it to me to just ask for them myself. But she played it off perfectly and then called from the back of the plane up to the crew in front to let them know the fish had been handed off.

When we landed, the pilot had even created a congratulatory certificate that had the coordinates of where we were (somewhere over Palm Springs) when the call from the flight attendant was heard in the cockpit "Swedish fish in hand." B had also arranged for my parents to be there waiting when we got off the plane. I'm pretty sure when they saw my face they knew this time was different. This was happening. Their girl was in love.

Chapter 7:
Sinatra Says it All

Me: I'm actually happy right now.
Life: LOL one sec.—**Unknown**

Getting married in a Mormon temple is typically a relatively small event. Members of the church have to follow high standards of worthiness to be able to enter the temple once it's been dedicated, and the "sealing rooms," where weddings are performed, typically hold no more than 30-40 people. Our wedding seemed overflowing to me as I looked into the faces of so many people I loved. All of my seven closest college roommates were there, and it seemed as though every one of our immediate and extended family members had made the effort to be there as well. It was amazing. The reception was the party I'd hoped it would be. Since our families had known each other for so long and still lived in relatively close proximity, the reception was like a huge reunion of our childhood. So many people were there from over the years and everyone was so excited to see our families combining. It was glorious. It was my fairy tale. Maybe there was such a person as Prince Charming after all.

Shortly after we met, B sent me a CD that he had burned of various songs. But there was something different about it. Rather than the song titles written on the cover, he had written phrases about each song, so I had to listen to the songs to see what each phrase meant. I thought it was one of the coolest things I'd ever seen. During our 18-month long-distance relationship, we exchanged many of these CD mixes, each time finding cute themes and funny or meaningful descriptions for each song. I distinctly remember being in the car with my parents with a new CD mix in hand. As we listened, Frank Sinatra's "Fly Me to the Moon" came on. If you don't know how that song ends, well . . . you should. I was pretty sure that was his way of telling me he loved me. I'd later browbeat it out of him for confirmation, but the butterflies that went crazy when I heard that song play were a beacon of hope to my tortured tummy. This guy was wickedly smart, incredibly witty, completely hilarious, and had just found a most creative way to tell me he loved me. What more could a girl ask for?

Lesson Learning: Life is full of if-onlys. Make the most of every moment, but accept that you can't change the past.

I wanted to tell my insecurities to hit the road. There wasn't room for both of us anymore. If only I could have made that so. Life's if-onlys result in some of the most painful regrets imaginable. But despite what the future held, that moment with Sinatra remains frozen in time as one of the happiest moments of my life.

Chapter 8:
From Cracks to Chasms

The truth is, it's hard to get people to like you, but it's even harder to keep people liking you.
—**Mindy Kaling**

I've had two broken noses, one from catching a pop fly with my face during a softball game in grad school and the other thinking I could try a surfboard behind my sister's boat, only to have it split my nose open and break it yet again . . . for my 40th birthday. I've had a myriad of stitches and a broken arm. All these I took in stride. But nothing could have prepped me for a broken marriage.

I had married B with the hopes that being around a happy person would make me happy. But soon into the marriage, I realized the dark clouds that hung around in my brain were still there. The worst part was that now I had someone onto whom I could project them. I watched B settle into married life and I felt like I didn't fit in. I was still traveling Mon-Fri and he worked Tues-Sat. Sundays were our only days together which typically involved church and then me getting ready to leave again the next day. Looking back I don't know if that hurt our relationship or prolonged it, but I felt distance creeping between us.

One of our most unique wedding gifts was my sister's dog, Tatum. My sister had moved from Arizona to Utah with her "outside" dog and felt horrible keeping him outside during the winters there. B had a dog, but shortly before he and I reconnected he had to put his dog down. I'd never owned a dog, but it seemed like adopting Tatum was something I could do for both my sister and my new husband. Tatum literally drove away with us after our wedding as we headed back to the central coast of California to B's apartment, our apartment, my new home.

We struggled to keep Tatum enclosed in the yard as he was not adjusting well to the transition. He would stiffen up and bare his teeth if we got near him. That lasted for a couple of months. He would also get out of the yard, and being in a new place, he struggled to find his way home. On one of those occasions just after we had arrived at our new life, we split up to look for Tatum. Across the street from us was a house for sale that we could tell must have an awesome view of Monterey Bay. Just for fun B and I decided to go to the open house. Since it had been agreed that I would be the one who handled the finances, B asked if we could afford it. I still owned my condo in southern California and had also flipped an investment in Arizona to a condo just 15 minutes north from where we were living that was supposed to eventually become our home.

But I knew B wanted this house. And I wanted to give it to him. When I looked at our finances, I told him we could do it but it would be incredibly tight. He wasn't worried. He could handle that. A mere 62 days after our wedding, we closed on the house. Given that I was traveling, B did all the moving. He had just moved me from Huntington Beach but with his ever happy disposition, he moved our stuff by himself across the street to our new home.

The first sign of worry for me was when the lender called me to ask if I knew what B's credit score was. I had no idea. I'd never seen him use a credit card, only a debit card. He never seemed too worried about money and although he admitted that he wasn't great with it, he was in total agreement with me being in charge, and I was fierce about money. I figured all would be well. When she told me the credit score my jaw dropped. I'd never heard of a credit score that low. I'd prided myself on keeping mine as high as possible. His was half of mine. It was the first glimpse I had that he might have an "irresponsible" side that I hadn't seen, and it scared me. Money was my security. Growing up without much had created a bit of a monster in me. As the oldest, I was greatly affected by the difficult financial situation my parents faced and carried that into my adult life, which has been both a blessing and a curse. Feeling like I had just hitched my wagon to someone who didn't seem to be as concerned with money matters was unnerving and alarming. It felt like the first little crack in our foundation. But I knew how badly he wanted the house. And I knew how badly I wanted to give it to him. So I financed the house by myself. I was now the sole financier on three houses, and although I didn't let on just how much, I was stressed. But B had cheerfully agreed to be the "property manager" so once again I felt the safety of his partnership and his commitment to me and to us.

Six months into the marriage I was struggling intensely. I was unhappy and felt that he had stopped trying, that I had become more like a roommate. I felt trapped. He agreed to counseling. I've always respected him for being willing to go to counseling. I've heard that many men will not admit that their relationship needs help or that they need help. But B said he wanted to do whatever it took to make me happy so we sought help. We entered counseling with two different objectives, however. He hoped the counseling would make me happy in the marriage. I hoped the counselor would point out that he needed to try harder to show me he loved me because I no longer believed that he really did. After all, I had asked him for the things I needed, yet those were never the things he did. What I didn't realize until later was that he was trying to tell me in his own way, the way he would have wanted to be shown. We were speaking two different languages and I think we both hoped the counselor would be the great translator. We were in counseling for 2 ½ of our 3 years of marriage. Sadly, there was no great translator. There was only me, desperate to feel a connection again to this man I married and him, hoping that I would find a way out of whatever I was struggling with and discover happiness and joy in my life.

One night in a sweet gesture that I will never forget, he asked me to grab my coat and come out on the balcony with him. As we stood there in the evening mist, he talked about the streetlight on the corner near our house. He talked about how he could look at it and find happiness in the beauty it provided. He could look around at the view and find joy in what he saw. He told me he wanted me to be able to have that too. Such a sweet gesture. But I just wanted him to tell me he thought I looked pretty when I dressed up, to hug me when he came home like he was happy to see me, to want to talk to me rather than just sit and watch TV with me. I wanted him to want me again like he had when we were dating. He would swear that nothing had changed. I would swear that everything had changed. He was slipping away from me.

One year into our marriage, I lost my job. As the primary breadwinner and with three mortgages in my name, I was scared to death. I later realized that B's love language was gifts. However, spending money was like fingernails on a chalkboard for me. He was in a Catch-22. But he continued to try showing his love in the best way he knew how. Because he was in the clothing business and knew the importance of proper attire, he bought me a beautiful suit to interview in and had a couple of shirts made for me. When I found a position open at the local community hospital that I was less than qualified for, he arranged with one of his high-end clients who had been on the hospital's board to meet with me and then put in a good word on my behalf. I'm forever grateful for that gesture because years after getting the job, my boss would tell me that although he was annoyed that the CEO was telling him who he should interview, he felt obligated and went ahead with the interview. He also told me that he would not have chosen to interview me based solely on my résumé. B had saved me again.

During my time between full-time jobs, B also encouraged me to do something I'd always wanted to do, and that was to get a job at the airport. I was able to get the full-time training done while unemployed and then continue the airport job part-time after getting hired by the hospital. The job provided great flight benefits. B and I could both fly free, and I could get my parents to Monterey for a visit rather inexpensively. But working two jobs was tough. I was exhausted. I would wake up and leave before he was up in the mornings and often I would come home after a late shift at the airport and slip into bed after he was already asleep. Either that or I would come home exhausted after the day job and go to bed long before he did. Shortly after starting my airport job, Tatum suddenly passed away. One night B was looking out the bedroom window and wanted me to come see the funny position Tatum had gone to sleep in on the pathway in the backyard. It took only moments for us to realize his eyes were still open. He was gone.

I felt an overwhelming sadness and guilt. I had spent the first year of our marriage being gone 5 days a week and was often too tired to get Tatum out on Saturdays. My sister had entrusted me with her pet that she'd had since he was a puppy and I had let him die. I was angry at B, thinking he hadn't spent as much time with Tatum as he could have while I was gone. I was devastated. When we took Tatum to the emergency vet, I asked to have a moment alone with him. I hugged him tightly and sobbing my eyes out, I told him I was sorry. I told my sister I was sorry. And I put another wedge between B and me.

The next year B was called into the corporate office of the job that he loved and was laid off.

Once again I completely freaked out about trying to make ends meet without having his income. At first, it was easy to be encouraging and to be a good partner during this rough time for him, but as the months continued, I felt more and more alone.

Right after he lost his job, he wanted to go see his old friends in Tucson, AZ where he had lived for 15 years before moving to Monterey. Looking back, I realize this was the beginning of the end. It's odd how you can get feelings about things but not realize their meaning until later. When he returned from Tucson I noticed he had a new Facebook friend. B had tons of Facebook friends and many of them were female. But I had an odd feeling when I saw this one. At the time, I shoved it aside. I often wonder if I hadn't done that, would things have turned out differently?

After 8 months of unemployment, B was finally going to be starting a new job shortly after the new year of 2010. It was late in 2009, and I was hopeful that 2010 would be a better year for us. After all, in the first 3 years of our marriage we had purchased a home we really couldn't afford, we had both lost jobs we cared about, our dog had died, and I had spent a year of the marriage working out of town and the rest of it working 2 jobs. We had been through a lot, and although divorce had been casually mentioned, somehow I felt that it just wasn't an option. We were committed to this. I so completely believed in his commitment to me that I felt like if anyone were to ask for a divorce it would be me and I wasn't going to do that. So I was in complete disbelief when after spending a week with what he said were his guy friends, he came home on New Year's Day of 2010 and once again changed the course of my life forever.

Lesson Learning: *God grant me the serenity to accept the things I cannot change, the courage to change the things I can, and the wisdom to know the difference.*—**Reinhold Niebuhr**

I was working the flight he came in on and he waved from the plane window as I martialed it in. I gave him a hug as he got off and told him I'd be home soon. When I got home he was eating at the kitchen table and I sat with him. When he finished he asked if we could sit on the couch and talk. With tears in his eyes, he told me he "couldn't do this anymore." My mind began swirling so fast I didn't even know what he meant. I asked if there was someone else. He vehemently denied it. Then he said, "I thought you'd be relieved." I was floored by that. How could I be relieved? Had he really thought I was so unhappy that I would just say good riddance to him? I couldn't breathe. I couldn't think. I could only cry.

He informed me that he was leaving in 5 days to go on a work trip and that he would be returning to Tucson after that. I knew there was something, someone in Tucson. I remembered the Facebook girl. She had once again appeared in a picture posted from this last trip with his friends. He had told me his guy friends were taking him to the Holiday Bowl in San Diego for his birthday. But there had been a picture of his friends at the game that didn't stay posted for long. And there she was in the picture. My mind flew to the phone conversation we had had on New Years' Eve when he was driving back from San Diego to Tucson. I was angry with him for not following up on money owed us from his former employer. He was angry that I was hounding him again about money. He told me he couldn't talk while he was with his friends. He had always been able to talk around his friends before. I remembered at the time thinking that was weird as well, but assuming it was mainly out of his anger.

The next 5 days after his declaration were some of the worst of my life. I called in sick to work. I didn't want to leave his side. I was desperate to change his mind, to make him see that we were not hopeless. "There is nothing that can change that would make me happy in the marriage. There is nothing you can do that would make me happy. People can't change who they are." Those words were piercing to me. I didn't want to believe them but somewhere deep down I wondered if he was right. I could feel the cold set in over those 5 days. He was desperate to leave. I was desperate to hold onto him. I was stunned at how quickly he could turn off feelings, like turning off a light switch. I didn't realize he'd been dimming the switch for months and this was just the final snuff out. He would try to tell me that this was hard for him too, but the only evidence of anything hard was him trying to survive the last 5 days with me before he could reach freedom. Later he would tell me the idea of coming to the house again made him physically sick. I could only interpret that as *I* made him physically sick. How had this happened? Somehow the tiny cracks had become a huge chasm, and I was now free falling into the void.

One of the most painful parts was the day he actually left. I took him to the airport (he was still flying for free on my flight benefits and would continue to do so for more than a year). I was heartbroken and crying as I watched him go through security. Although as an airline employee, I could go through with him if I wanted, I couldn't bear the anguish of sitting there and waiting for him to get on the plane. But I stayed at the airport. After his flight left, a coworker of mine at the airport came to check on me. She was visibly angry and finally told me that after he had gone through security he had found a seat and gotten on the phone. He had cheerfully chatted and laughed on the phone while waiting to board. She had seen me on the other side of security and couldn't believe that someone who was leaving his wife could have been so cavalier. Waves of nausea rolled over me. During the next few weeks when I would think I couldn't possibly be hurt any more than I already had been, I would find more and more evidence of his interactions with the woman in Tucson.

About a month later I had concrete proof that they had been carrying on a relationship in some form for at least a couple of months before he left me. Going to Tucson meant going to be with her. Today they are still together. Their relationship has already outlasted the time it took us to date, be married, and finalize a divorce. Even now, that fact can still cause pain, especially if I let myself wallow in the part I played in his decision to leave. But with his departure, I finally realized that I couldn't keep living my life so broken all the time. I wanted to prove to him, and to myself, that I could change. I had to. Thus began a new journey. It was a journey through the stages of grief, through the most intense regret my mind could imagine, through self-discovery, through a refiner's fire, and through another major life crisis I didn't see coming.

Chapter 9:
Wild Animal

Someday you're gonna look back on this moment of your life as such a sweet time of grieving. You'll see that you were in mourning and your heart was broken, but your life was changing . . .
—Elizabeth Gilbert

I've spent some time over the last several years having it out with God and trying to figure out just what the heck He was doing. I wasn't angry with Him that B left. But I was angry because I felt alone and abandoned by Him. I had no family nearby and no close friends. I was far from home and B had gone back to his safety net and into the arms of someone else. I had never felt so rejected. I had never felt worse about myself. I could feel myself slipping into the abyss that I had fallen into when I was left by myself in that first nursing home. This pain felt unsurvivable. I knew people got through this kind of excruciating pain, but I couldn't for the life of me figure out how. I was so desperate for the pain to ease, for the waves of grief and nausea to subside, for my mind to not go to terrible places.

I tried to function at work but made some huge mistakes during that time, especially the week in March when B came into town for the sole purpose of filing for divorce. There was no more discussion to be had. The light had been switched to off and I had been left in the dark. Whatever pain he may have experienced, he hid it well and I began to feel that he was patronizing me as he would assure me that I was a strong woman and would get through this.

How does anyone get through this? I had hoped that maybe he'd come back, that maybe he'd realize that he had made promises, that he still loved me, that he just needed some time apart to work through some things. But probably to my benefit, there was no waffling. As painful and awful as that was, I can only imagine how much worse and prolonged it might have been if he had tried to keep one foot on either side. But to watch him go, without having to spend a single night alone and walk straight into the arms of a blonde who shared his love of golf and baseball made me feel inferior and small. I wasn't enough. That poor little girl from my not-so-distant past who made herself sick trying to get others to notice and value her, had just suffered the biggest blow of her life. The person she had shared all her vulnerabilities with had rejected her, had left her, had fallen out of love with her. The only thing I can imagine that would be worse would be the rejection of parent to child and thankfully, I've never had to experience that. I have always had complete love and support from my parents. But they were far away and without the means to get to me. I began to literally waste away.

The divorce diet is by far the most effective one I've ever experienced. I lost 25 pounds in just 2 months. But along with that loss came the loss of globs of hair and what felt like a complete loss of my soul and any and all personality. I prayed to God to rescue me from this. My rescuer was gone now. It was interesting because I could see that God was sending other people into my life. In complete and utter desperation, I began to reach out to others to keep myself from completely holing up in my house. As with the nursing home, I knew if there was ever a day I let myself stay in bed I would never get up again. So I kept getting up.

Most people would say having kids makes going through divorce and dealing with the aftermath more difficult. They are probably right. But I literally only had myself to get up for in the morning. And if the person who was supposed to know me the best placed so little value on me, how could I place value on myself? At least that's where my mind went.

Lesson Learning: There is no way around grief, only through it. Let the grief come out.

Grief is an interesting beast. Sometimes the valleys are so low you're sure you are worse off than where you started. I remember a coworker/friend who had been through a divorce that involved her ex ending up in a relationship with another woman. She became a sounding board for me even though it seemed she got through her grief much faster than I was getting through mine. One day she said, "Just wait till you cry like a wild animal."

"What? Not me." I was pretty sure I wasn't even capable of that.

"Just wait. You will. Just wait," she said. Months later I found out exactly what she meant.

After a particularly difficult day emotionally and another torturous evening of scouring

Facebook, something inside me just cracked. I fell to the floor and started to weep. This had happened plenty of times over the months so I just braced myself for it. But as the sorrow, regret, hurt, and pain rolled over me, I could hardly breathe from the tightness in my chest. And then it happened. I heard the most guttural, primitive sound come out of me. It was a sound I didn't even realize a human could make. It was the cry of a wild animal. I had never cried like that before and I've never cried like it since. But I'll never forget it. The fear, pain and vulnerability had overcome my body. I was cracked open.

Chapter 10:
Desperate Times

It's amazing how someone can break your heart and you can still love them with all the little pieces.—**Anonymous**

Over the months after B's departure, and as I watched his communication become even colder and more distant, I was desperate for comfort. I was desperate for someone or something. I was the loneliest I had ever been. But I was also the angriest, the most hurt, the most disappointed, and the most regretful. I literally experienced the "most" of every negative emotion I could possibly imagine. I couldn't eat. I couldn't sleep. I couldn't function at work. I couldn't engage in conversations very well. How could he leave me? How could he make me trust him and believe him, make promises to me, and then leave when it got too hard? How could he give up on me? On us? On our vows? How could he run to someone else? I knew I was going crazy, literally driven to madness. I had to fight the urge every day, if not every minute, every second to not shrivel in a corner somewhere and weep.

I needed to pull through this. I couldn't crumble. I couldn't roll over and let him be right about me. I had to show him that people can change, that I could change. I didn't know where else to start but with trying to make some friends. Because I had traveled for work for most of the time we'd lived in the area, I hardly knew a soul. I knew a few people from church and had a couple of coworkers I worked closely with, but that was it. So I started looking for friends. And in some cases, I did whatever it took no matter how it looked. At one point I signed up for exercise classes that my employer offered. The girl who taught the classes seemed nice. One day after class, I waited behind to talk to her. In my awkward way, I basically said, "You seem really nice. Wanna hang out and be friends?" Thankfully and miraculously she agreed. Upon leaving her home the first night she invited me over, in a neighborhood with no streetlights, I high-centered my car on a boulder that was part of her landscape. After staring at it in horror for several minutes, I had to knock on her door and ended up having to sleep over until her husband, who worked nights, could get home in the morning and figure out what to do. There's nothing like an unexpected sleepover to solidify a new friendship.

I forced myself to go to a party at my neighbor's house, a fate worse than death as far as I was concerned. But I met a guy there who eventually became one of my closest friends. I forced myself to talk to people at church, even if all I could say was hi. It felt like some of the hardest work I had ever done. But it had to be done. I was on a mission to prove B wrong, and to save my own life.

I went to a divorce support group at a local church. I was so nervous yet so desperate for help. I remember during the first night of introductions we went around the room and most in the group were either contemplating divorce, currently in the process of separation or divorce or recently divorced. Then one lady introduced herself and said she got divorced in 1989. My first thought was "God help me if I still need a divorce support group after 20 years!" But the further I got in the recovery process, the more I understood that some of the wounds may never completely heal. We just do our best to not pick at them and aggravate them. But sometimes we are left with a void, and sometimes that void doesn't get filled in the way we'd like or even at all. But there was a valuable lesson here.

Lesson Learning: Divorce leaves a void, but a fulfilling life doesn't necessarily require that the void be filled.

I read so many self-help and divorce books over those first few years that I basically have my own library. Sometimes I still walk by my bookcase and laugh at the thought of someone visiting and perusing my books to look for a good read. They'd have the choice of titles such as *Falling Apart in One Piece*, *How to Survive the Loss of a Love*, *Recovering from Divorce: Overcoming the Death of a Dream*, or my personal favorite, *Divorced, Drunk, & Covered in Cat Hair*. Combine these with all the depression, dysthymia, anxiety, and stress reduction books, the books on finding peace through spirituality, and the business and finance books I'd collected over the years in my quest to become rich, and they'd have the picture of one utterly discontent person. That bookcase reveals a tortured little soul trying to find peace, contentment, purpose, meaning, and fulfillment, a self-help junkie just trying to make sense of it all and find happiness, hope, and excitement. I suppose I shouldn't leave out my small Dr. Seuss collection. There's a reason he's called a doctor.

One thing I noticed in most of the best-selling books involving a divorce and a rediscovery was that these women (yes, it seems only women write books about their own divorce) did something huge to find themselves. And in the end, they often found happiness in other romantic relationships. I was feeling even more convinced that in order to prove my worth to B, to myself, and to the world at large, I needed to go "Eat, Pray, Love" myself into a journey of self-discovery and romance. There was only one problem. Well, two. One, I didn't have the luxury of running away from my life. And two, I knew full well I wasn't ready for a relationship. All I really wanted was for B to admit he'd made a mistake. Sadly, when I had asked him as he was leaving how he could do this and didn't he remember the good memories from not so long ago, his response had been swift and cutting, "That wasn't reality. This is reality."

Lesson Learning: Moving forward means turning away from a closed door

and discovering there is life ahead of you.

In his mind, the mistake was the marriage. There would be no coming back. But for me, how could there be a moving forward? Moving forward, I would come to learn, did not necessarily mean another relationship, at least not a romantic relationship. It meant a relationship with myself. And I couldn't afford to run away to a foreign country or the Pacific Crest Trail to do it. If I really wanted to become like B, the man who loved life and was always happy, the only person who could create that was me. But how was I supposed to stop obsessing about him, his new car, his new job, and his girlfriend so that I could have a chance to find myself?

Someone once gave me the analogy that what I was doing by obsessing about B and his life was the equivalent of staring at, with my nose nearly planted on, a closed door. He and his new life were on the other side. The door was locked. I couldn't get into their life. But if I just turned around, I could see that I was in my own beautiful life. I kept trying to turn around and feeling like all I was seeing was what I had lost. It was time for more drastic measures.

Chapter 11:
Surfer Ken

If someone breaks your heart just punch them in the face. Seriously. Punch them in the face and go get some ice cream.—**Frank Ocean**

When B and I were in counseling, the counselor asked us to get a Ken doll (of Barbie & Ken fame) and bring it to a session. B dutifully went and bought "Surfer Ken." That seemed an appropriate choice if Ken were to represent B, as he had taken up surfing and unemployment had only increased his opportunity to practice. It would be one of the many things that I understood too late about B. He dealt with stress differently than I did. Surfing was an escape to clear his head and give him time to think and plan. To me, it seemed a way to avoid looking for a job, and it was both frustrating and hurtful as I would come home from my second job at the airport and he would ask that I shower before bed because I smelled like the airplane lavatory. I was exhausted and just wanted to lay my head down and be appreciated for keeping the household afloat. I didn't realize at the time that maybe it was hard for him to express appreciation while experiencing the roller coaster of my emotions. Outwardly, I was trying to support him, while inside, the anger, frustration, and hurt were bubbling up and would sometimes erupt out of nowhere. I would later get a glimpse of what it must have been like for him to be unsure of who would come home each night, friend or foe, but that was hindsight.

As it turned out, B and I never learned the purpose of Surfer Ken. We never made it that far. A year after he left, my good friend who had warned me about the wild animal cry invited me to join her and her daughter on a Mediterranean cruise. It was to be my post-divorce "I'm moving on" trip; however the divorce wasn't yet final. Minor detail. I hoped at the least it would be a distraction from the pain and sadness, and I had a plan for Ken.

Lesson Learning: Moving forward isn't linear, and change is often imperceptible

In some of my self-help books I had heard about "separation rituals." Surfer Ken had a new purpose. He was coming with me to the Mediterranean and when the time was right, he was going to represent B and I was going to say goodbye by chucking Ken off the stern of the ship and watching him sink to the bottom of the sea. I wrote my goodbye to B, naming all the things I wanted to be free from, all the things I wanted to say, and then one night during the cruise, I left my room just after 11 p.m. and went to the outdoor seating area on the back of the ship. I sat in the darkness at one of the tables near the railing and said a tearful goodbye to Surfer Ken. This was an awkward thing to do on a cruise ship, even at 11 p.m. I had waited until that hour to have the least chance of being seen having an emotional breakup with a doll, but still there were a few times I had to shove Ken in my bag as someone walked nearby. When I didn't get Ken back in the bag soon enough, I got some really priceless looks. Finally after my best attempts at a thorough goodbye, at 11:37 p.m. somewhere between Istanbul & Malta, I stuck Ken's hand through the Ziploc holding my written goodbye and I threw him into the sea. (Sorry environmentalists, but it was a necessary evil.)

I watched him descend and hit the water, then the darkness was too much to follow him so I watched where I thought he was. Then I wrote in my notebook. "Ken/B is overboard. I'm free.

My life awaits me and I'm going to embrace it. I'm going to be in the moment on the rest of this cruise and I'm going to find hope in my present and future. I will find happiness within myself by learning how to speak positively. I will take the lessons I learned from B about loving life and embrace them. I will continue to change, but for myself. B is gone. B was my past. I am my future."

I expected to feel some kind of magical change in my heart at that moment, and although it felt good, I felt only partial relief. It was as if despite being physically separated from him, no matter what I tried, I was unable to feel psychologically separated. This was another of many times when I realized that healing takes time and the amount of time isn't necessarily determined by us. We can write letters, chuck Ken dolls, yell and scream into pillows, punch punching bags, and try a myriad of other "coping skills," but in the end, our healing time is our healing time and there is no magic strategy to end it. We might dull the pain of it, or possibly even speed it up a bit, but it passes in frustratingly tiny, imperceptible increments. The point is, it passes.

Chapter 12:
Don't Deny the Denial

It's not denial. I'm just selective about the reality I accept.—**Bill Waterson**

I remember learning about the five stages of grief (denial, anger, bargaining, depression, and acceptance) in my college psychology course but no one ever explained that you don't just move through them sequentially, checking each one off the list upon completion and moving on to the next. Oh no, you can bounce back and forth like a pinball between anger and bargaining or wallow in depression for months, only to find yourself plopped back into denial. There is nothing linear about grief.

Well-meaning friends and family however, believe they know exactly what you need to do. Even those who have been through the same experiences can make you feel like what worked for them should work for you. Maybe they have some valid points and maybe I "should have" been over it in six months, but my takeaway looking back is that I spent a lot of time beating myself up for not being "over it" in this "suggested" six-month timeframe. For me, it happened and continues to happen organically, on a timeframe that I don't always have as much control over as I would like. Sure, maybe I've spent way too much time swimming in denial but I am learning to own my process, denial and all. And as Miranda Lambert sings, "This ain't my mama's broken heart." Okay, I might be trying to justify the amount of time I spent in denial and how I may still bounce back into it from time to time. But I make no claims to be the poster child for quick healing. What I do know however, is that feeling that little bit of life creep back into your soul is worth the wait. That said, I definitely have had, and continue to have my share of grieving and though I own my process, I have spent a lot more time in denial than I like to admit.

Lesson Learning: The five stages of grief don't always occur sequentially and the denial stage is the hardest to accept.

When I attended the divorce support group, the facilitator introduced himself and told his story. He had been divorced, but five years later he remarried his ex and they were now blissfully happy. In my opinion, having him as a group leader just created a huge cesspool of denial to swim in. I didn't understand how deep that muck was until I hit the five-year mark from when B told me he was leaving. It was as if something inside me said, "Time's up! It's been five years and he hasn't come back." I wish I could say that moment was like a light switch and I flipped the switch from "not healed" to "healed," but no such luck. However, that date was still pivotal. After having pushed on the flywheel for the last five years, the creaky old thing finally started to budge. I just had to get the momentum going. But would my flywheel have inched forward earlier if Mr. I-got-back-with-my-ex-after-five-years hadn't unintentionally fueled the hope that already existed in my denial-ridden mind? Maybe. Maybe not. But it did feel like some magic number to me.

My denial tire exploded when I came across an article one day about Marie Osmond. I had been a huge Donny & Marie fan as a child. The article said that after 25 years, Marie was remarrying her first husband to whom she had been married for the same amount of time as B and me. And the kicker, she was going to wear the same wedding dress. Deep denial confession ahead: I called my mom and only half-jokingly told her to scrap any thoughts she had of getting rid of my dress that still hung in my closet at home. I didn't care if it took up a ton of space. If it could happen for Marie, then it was possible for me! I had to be prepped and ready with dress in hand! There's no denying, denial sucks. Especially in hindsight.

As kids, misbehavior got us sent to our rooms. Oftentimes as we were sobbing hysterically from our room, we would hear, "You can come out when you're happy." My sister's response was classic. She'd stand in the doorway of our room and, still sobbing uncontrollably, she'd yell, "I happy! I happy!" It was a pathetic attempt that I never understood and my parents didn't even acknowledge. But as I look back over my email correspondence with B during my plethora of denial phases, I felt just like my little sis. I was trying so hard to show that I had changed, that what had driven him away was fixed, that I had figured out how to be happy. As I read my pleading attempts to get him to reconsider, I could almost hear my own voice hysterically screaming, "I happy! I happy!" Just like my parents reacted toward my sister, B didn't buy it. Not only that but as time lapsed and my perspective changed, I would read those emails and feel even more of the chill in his responses, more of his firmness as he shut down my pleadings, and even more of the desperation oozing from my attempts to appear happy. My nose had been so firmly pressed against the door he had shut that I somehow believed if I just kept knocking, he would eventually open the door to my death-bed repentance efforts. Silly girl. Pained girl. Girl in denial.

Chapter 13:
Sentimental Stuff

When the past calls, let it go to voicemail. It's got nothing new to say.—Unknown

Years after his departure, I found a book on depression that B had read, highlighted with notes in the margins about how he could use what he was learning in the book to help me gain insights into what was happening to me and help me find my way out of the darkness, a way to heal. There was another similar book with a note he had penciled in on the first page, "We can do this! I love you!" These were beautiful signs of what had once been his hope. Finding and reading these evidences of his past love just ripped my heart open again.

I can't say this enough: heartbreak is not just one big blow and then recovery. Over the months and years after he left, things like finding this book continued to sabotage me and I was gutted over and over again. It felt like the times when as a little girl, we would go to the beach in the summers and in my attempts to body surf, sometimes I'd get swallowed by a wave. Coughing and choking, I'd manage to get to the surface only to be knocked down by the next wave in the set. Starting to feel absolutely desperate to get air and panicked that the waves would never stop, I was afraid that I would eventually be swallowed by the sea and taken out by the second thing on my list of most feared ways to die.

We all have moments when we feel like we're fighting for our life against monster waves. But when the waves hit, although seemingly counterintuitive, your best chance for survival is just to relax and not fight the wave. Let yourself go limp and go with the flow of the water. Inherently we struggle and flail against the wave, not realizing that the more we fight it, the more we get pushed under and eventually become exhausted from the struggle.

Inevitably, all of us face potentially destructive waves throughout our lives. The key is learning how to arm ourselves mentally, emotionally, and physically. Accept the natural rhythm and flow of life and when the wave hits, stop fighting to get your head above the water for a moment and be assured that the wave will pass and you'll float to the surface as you have in times past. This one adjustment on your part could be the point where you stop fearing the waves in your future and open yourself up to replace the time spent in dreaded anticipation of the next onslaught, with time spent enjoying the calm between waves.

But as I didn't know this then, I was overwhelmed by wave after wave of heartbreaks. In this terribly nonlinear and unpredictable wave set, the heartbreaks seemed to just keep coming. Heartbreak #1, him telling me he was leaving. Heartbreak #2, him laughing on the phone in the airport the day he left me. Heartbreak #3, finding out there was someone else. Heartbreak #4, when he came into town to file for divorce. When I was sure I had suffered the worst of the blows, along came Heartbreak #5.

Since music was always a big part of our relationship, it became both my solace and my pain after he was gone. Every song started to have some meaning. At one point after he left, I even gave him another CD just like the ones that brought us together, with phrases rather than titles to identify the songs. It was meant to have the overarching theme that I was okay but if he wanted me back I'd be there. Strangely I can't remember the title I gave it. If it had been up to me I'd still have the paper where I wrote down the title and playlist with the myriad of scribbles trying to find just the right words that would soften his heart. But that paper is gone. Part of Heartbreak #5.

Lesson Learning: Sentimental stuff, if not thrown away, should at least be packed away.

After an intervention by my friends where they came over and pulled everything down that had anything to do with B and boxed it up while I sobbed, I decided to continue packing his stuff to get it out of the house and into the garage. The things my friends had taken down became my "sentimental" box and I labeled it as such. I put everything in there. The framed pictures of us that served as our guest book with signatures all over the matting, all the CDs we had made for each other, every note, card, and letter he had ever written, even the brown paper bag he had turned into wrapping paper and drawn pictures on, and of course the playlist from my last CD. Nearly every evidence that he had ever loved me was in that box. Only my ring remained tucked away in a safe in the house. I would later thank God I hadn't put it in the "sentimental" box.

I'm a pack rat to a certain extent, at least about sentimental things. As I mentioned before, I literally have every note or letter that has ever been written to me since third grade. Every time I've thought about getting rid of them, I start to go through them and am reminded why I keep them. They are proof. Proof that boys had crushes on me, proof that I was desirable, proof that someone wanted me, proof that someone picked me, proof that to someone at some point, I was their first choice.

After putting all of B's stuff in the garage, I rarely went in there. Little by little, he came and took it all away. One day, months later, I came across something that I wanted to put in the "sentimental" box. I went to the garage and couldn't find the box anywhere. A sick feeling came over me. He had probably thought it was one of his and taken it with him. I had to have it back. I was desperate. It was the only evidence that what he was telling me now about the marriage being a mistake was a lie, all the evidence that he had really and truly loved me, all the evidence that validated the last few years of my life with him. It was my only proof. I had to have it.

Any necessary communications at that point were done through email. But I couldn't write and wait for his answer. I was a mess. As much as it pained me, I called him and asked him if he had taken it. He had indeed taken it, but when I asked for it back, he simply said, "I threw it out." Another wave hit me. More coughing and choking. More panic that I couldn't get air. As much as I wanted him to believe I had changed, like I had been preaching to him since the minute he told me he couldn't do "this" anymore, my façade cracked and I began to cry. The voice that came out of me next was squeaky and weak, devastated beyond belief. "You threw it away? But you know me. You know how sentimental I am." I couldn't stop the tears or the sound of complete anguish in my voice. I couldn't even try to show him feigned bravery or how "changed" I was. "How could you not have called and asked me if I had really meant to get rid of it? How . . . could . . . you?" My head was spinning. This couldn't really be happening.

"I'm sorry," he said. It was one of the few times after he left that I heard any emotion in his voice. I knew he meant it. "I thought you were trying to tell me something," he continued. "That it didn't mean anything to you. My apartment is small and I had to get rid of a lot of things, and I figured if it didn't mean anything to you . . ." It didn't matter what he said at that point. It was all gone. Every tangible piece of evidence. Everything but my ring. I was so grateful I had that ring tucked away. At that point, it was all I had left. My only proof that my fairy tale had been real. I'd love to say I eventually chucked it off the boat with Surfer Ken or pawned it, but it still sits safely tucked away . . . because I still love that ring. I love what it represented. I love the promise that it carried. Someday, I may be able to part with it. Someday I may not need that proof anymore. Someday my own knowledge that it was real may be all the proof I need. But I am a work in progress. I am healing, not healed. But I am healing.

Chapter 14:
I Don't Do Pink

Experience is what you get when you don't get what you want.—Tori Filler

It was January 17, 2012, and I was sitting at work when Dr. Roux from the imaging center called me. I wasn't even worried about the call coming. I was certain that what I had found was just some type of cyst. I had asked the doctor about seemingly similar bumps on my body in the past and the response was always the same. "Those are just fat bumps that develop as we age." Wonderful. Apparently as we get older our fat deposits in bumps. Who knew? So I had stopped worrying about my "fat bumps" a long time ago. In no way did I expect to hear what came out of Dr. Roux's mouth. "I have bad news. The cells are cancerous." The room felt weird and I suddenly felt like I was floating outside my body. "Are you saying I have breast cancer?" I replied. My coworker whipped her head around, eyes wide as saucers. Her older sister had just died of breast cancer less than 3 months before. I didn't know what to say or do or think.

Dr. Roux told me to call my primary care doctor and get a referral for an oncologist. I had only ever met my primary care doctor one time before. During an annual exam, the nurse practitioner whom I normally saw called Dr. Wesley in to talk about the fact that if I wanted to have kids I might need to think about making that happen, since I was already at the age that would constitute a "geriatric" pregnancy. I was in my 30s for crying out loud! Apparently 30 is the new 80 when it comes to your ovaries. Dr. Wesley was a tall Black woman who was like a gust of air when she entered the room. She spoke in a loud, fast voice, and I could tell pretty quickly that most patients probably just did what they were told by Dr. Wesley.

At that first interaction, she walked into the room and immediately launched into the fact that I needed to stop my birth control that very minute, stop at the store on the way home and get pre-natal vitamins, and go home and get to work on making a baby. She explained how the odds of complications and birth defects increased dramatically with the mother's age and that I wasn't "getting any younger." I felt like I had just come to the top of one of those loopy roller coasters, as I sheepishly said,

"We're having some problems in our marriage. We're in counseling." "What?" she exclaimed. "Well, you forget everything I just said! All of it! You stay on that pill and you take it faithfully. No talk of babies here." And then she was gone. It was the only time I ever saw her.

When I called and left a message at Dr. Wesley's office for an oncologist recommendation, she called me back personally. She expressed concern for how I was doing and then got down to business. She told me the names of the doctors I would see for both oncology and surgery. I didn't ask any questions. I wasn't even sure I could formulate any.

Within 2 weeks I had an appointment with the oncologist. Dr. Ganales was a stern Russian woman with a thick accent. She scared the crap out of me. Dr. Wesley had said she was the best, but it was debatable as to what I was more scared of, her or cancer.

Lesson Learning: Stress can cause cancer. Be kind to your body.

As I sat in Dr. Stuntz's office, the surgeon who would perform three surgeries on me over the next several months, I couldn't help but feel that out-of-body sensation again. As I sat there in the exam gown, he drew on the paper that covered the exam table. He was describing how cancers typically form and the process of rapid multiplication. Then he said something that stopped me in my tracks. "Based on the size of the tumor, I'd say it's been growing for about two years."

My jaw dropped. "Can stress cause cancer?" I asked.

"There are definitely studies that show that it can be a causal factor."

"Like divorce?" I asked.

"Sure," he replied.

I couldn't believe it. I had received my diagnosis two years, two weeks, and two days after B had said he was leaving. I hadn't realized that the "divorce diet," the hair loss and all the other physical symptoms that wreaked havoc on me during those first few months after he left were weakening my immune system and had allowed cancer to develop in my body. I couldn't hold back. "You mean that jerk left me all alone in a place where I know no one, with three mortgages, all of which are upside down, and gave me BREAST CANCER?!"

As mad as I was, and I hate to admit this (like so many other parts of this experience I hate to admit), I thought maybe, just maybe, if he knew I had cancer he would at least talk to me. Maybe he would be worried. Maybe this would allow us to be friends. Maybe he would want to come back and take care of me. Maybe the possibility that I might not survive would help him realize he still loved me. I was wrong on all accounts.

Although I wanted him to believe that my death was a possibility, from the first moment I heard that I had cancer and throughout the entire process, I was never afraid that I would die. I'm not sure why that was. Maybe because my cancer was at a low stage. Maybe because I was too busy thinking about how this might bring B back into my life and give me some kind of street cred or badge of honor to wear. Or maybe because the me who was still being honest with myself believed somewhere deep down that death would be a welcome relief to the pain I was feeling. Whatever the reason, I never feared death. I didn't believe I deserved to escape my pain that easily.

What I did fear far more than death however, was being bald. I knew there was no way I could be divorced AND bald. I was 37 years old, which was way too close to 40 for comfort and, in my mind, already nearing the end of my "marketable" days. By the time it grew back to previous lengths, I'd be well into my 40s, and who would want me then? My long hair was my security blanket, my woobie, so no matter what else they wanted to do to me, I was not going to let them take my hair. When Doc Ganales told me, in her stern Russian way, that chemo was going to be part of the treatment, I completely crumbled. She basically told me I didn't really have a choice given that I was young and it was the most proven course of action against my type of cancer. I couldn't breathe. There had to be another way. After all, I was miserable. I didn't much care if I died. But I sure as heck couldn't stay alive and be bald. That seemed a little like facing death but without the end of the pain. No thank you.

It wasn't just about being bald either. It was about having short hair while it grew out. Guys like long hair. At least most of the ones I've encountered. So the thought of how long it would take to get back my long hair made me feel like I was sealing my single status for many years to come. In a twisted bit of foreshadowing, months before my diagnosis, my coworker who had lost her sister to cancer brought her wigs to donate. One of them was a short pixie-type cut. For fun, I had tried it on and sent a picture to my family and a few others telling them I had cut my hair. The responses were priceless. They had all tried to show support without revealing how awful I looked. At least not until I told them it was a joke. That was another reminder that I would never ever have short hair. Little did I know that just months later, I'd have to decide between short hair and assuaging my family's fear of me dying.

One of the downsides of being adored by your parents is that you know if you leave them prematurely, you're pretty much ending their lives as well. Despite my utterly terrifying fear of losing my hair, I didn't want my parents or my siblings, my nieces and nephews, or my last living grandparent to think they weren't worth putting up a fight for. Although I didn't believe death was on the table, I knew my family did. I was completely torn.

My focus up until that point had been to keep talking to professionals and reading research until I determined I was armed with enough info to tell Doc Ganales that I was standing up to her and choosing not to do chemo. Radiation, fine. Cutting out a piece of my already smaller boob, not ideal but fine. Even hormone therapy which would make it impossible for me to have a child until I finished a five-year regimen was something I could face. But not chemo. After facing my inadequacies in an incredibly intimate way over the last few years and now being faced with losing the primary asset I clung to in order to feel somewhat attractive, I didn't believe my damaged psyche would survive the trauma.

With cancer, everything is just a statistic, so from what I could tell, chemo wouldn't even buy me enough percentage points against recurrence to make it worth the experience anyway. And though the baldness was terrifying, the painted-on eyebrows, fake eyelashes, and scarves that scream "I have cancer" were just the icing on my hell-no cake. I walked into the cancer counselor's office the first time and adamantly told her I WOULD NOT be wearing pink, I WOULD NOT be putting pink ribbons on my car, I WOULD NOT be marching in 60-mile walks proudly wearing a pink scarf! I WAS NOT a warrior in pink! I was not one of them! (I believe it was at that point that she lovingly told me I wasn't ready to attend the support group yet. Apparently, I wouldn't have been a good influence on the other sick people.)

Chapter 15:
Don't Want to Miss Anything

Everything you want is on the other side of fear.
—Jack Canfield

I heard from B one time during my cancer treatment. We had some tax issues we still needed to take care of that involved him owing me some money that would be helpful for medical bills. Our tax preparer agreed to communicate with him about it and I told her it was okay to tell him I was having medical issues. I wanted him to know. I wanted him to care. A phone call finally came and in his ever-happy voice, he asked how I was doing. I told him I was fine, but I had already developed a terrible cold from the neighbor kid, and I was coughing like crazy on the phone. He probed some more and after stalling as much as I could to make myself seem more brave, I finally told him that I had breast cancer. Drawing out my news was also my way of trying to show him that I wasn't looking to drum up sympathy. But let's face it, that's exactly what I was hoping for.

He seemed genuinely concerned and I was so relieved to hear it in his voice. We had what I thought was a great conversation, and when we hung up, I was sure this had opened the door for us to communicate about something other than money. I saw a glimmer of hope that we might actually at least be friends after all, and maybe he'd be there to go through this with me. But I never heard from him again. I later would have to email him periodically over long, drawn-out, and frustrating divorce-related financial issues, to which I would receive very distant, business-like replies. But he never called me again, never initiated another email, never asked how I was doing. I was devastated. He really didn't love me anymore. Not only that, he didn't care enough about me to express any level of concern, or to look past any of our issues to realize that I was facing something scary and I was all alone. It was Heartbreak #6. Thankfully I wasn't entirely alone. It's weird to look back at situations and see how things came together for a reason. Some call it fate, some call it luck, some call it divine intervention. Whatever it was, I was grateful for it.

After Doc Ganales' crushing blow that meant I was facing baldness, I drove home to AZ for a weekend to be with my parents. Surprisingly without really ever making a conscious decision, it was there that the dial creaked slightly toward accepting chemo. For as long as I can remember since leaving home, I have always slept on the couch when I come to visit. Nearly every time, I get the same response from my parents. "Why don't you go sleep in your nice comfortable bed where you can close the door and get some rest?" For years I wasn't sure why I preferred the couch, but at some point it came to me. I didn't want to miss anything. I wanted to be sure I was in the middle of the action until the last person went to bed and when the first person woke up.

I spent time with my parents that weekend and spent the evenings looking at the sole string of Christmas lights that had been left in their kitchen window, which they had named "Tiff's Christmas Window of Healing." I felt the weight of the survival mode I'd been operating in for so many years lift for a moment.

While driving back to Monterey, I realized I had taken steps toward chemo. I had a wig that my parents had spent a fortune on to make sure I had something that made me feel pretty. For the first time in my life, I was going to be a blonde. I had cut my hair in an effort to make it less traumatic to lose while being able to donate it to someone else who would be having similar fears. And somewhere on that drive, it occurred to me why I had started to take those steps . . . I still didn't want to miss anything. Even today I'm not entirely sure what that "anything" is. Maybe a niece's wedding, a family member with a need that could be uniquely filled by me, being a friend to a scared cancer patient, finding that internal happiness and becoming a lover of life, an amazing marriage of my very own, following a dream, discovering a new dream, finding my calling, or just living in a way that would leave me on my death bed kicking and screaming, not wanting to go because of the awesome ride I was having.

Pessimistically, I thought if my next 37 years were going to be the "survival" experience of the last 37, I didn't really care to face the overwhelming fear of chemo for that. But there was that little part of me that thought, what if they weren't? What if this was a turning point, a refiner's fire that gave me the drive to do those little daily things that could lead to the big changes I was always longing for? Well, that would be one thing I wouldn't want to miss.

Chapter 16:
Humor & Needles

Lucy: Do you think you have Pantaphobia, Charlie Brown?
Charlie: I don't know, what is pantaphobia?
Lucy: The fear of Everything.
Charlie: THAT'S IT!!!
—Charles M. Schulz

As the reality continued to sink in that B was never coming back, I felt like I was fighting a seemingly never-ending battle to survive. As with my prior scary mental health issues, I knew if I didn't do something, I would curl up at home and never leave again. So as I mentioned before, I started to do what I could to make friends. Work friends, church friends, neighborhood friends. I needed people in my life who were close enough to realize if I was going down hard and hopefully swim out to save me.

Before cancer struck, I had done the best I felt capable of doing during the previous two years to nurture connections. And when I reached out to these newfound friends, they came running. I had friends to go to doctors' appointments with, friends to drive me to and from surgeries, friends who allowed me to take months off of work during treatment, friends who brought me meals, friends who sent me cards, and friends who visited me. I will forever be indebted to those friends. Yet when I crawled into bed each night, I was still painfully alone. Those were the times when the scary monsters of my childhood dreams would find their way into my head. Or worse, I would have sweet dreams of B's return, of loving intimacy between us, of the looks he used to give me when we were dating that made me feel like he would be with me forever. Then I would wake up, roll over with utter anticipation and realize the other side of the bed was empty. I still have never slept on his side.

Lesson Learning: When you have a serious illness, look for humor and you'll find it . . .then blog about it.

I realized soon after my diagnosis that it was important to family and friends to keep them up-to-date on how things were going. My dear friend from grad school had been diagnosed with a much more severe and rare form of breast cancer the year before me and her brother had started a Facebook page where she could post updates. I was too tired to talk to people on the phone, plus I've never been much of a phone person anyway. Interestingly one of the things I hate even more than phone conversations is writing. But I saw no other choice, so I began a blog. In the spirit of full disclosure, I had previously made fun of blogs. I had tons of friends who kept blogs but I never seemed to be able to find (translation: make) the time to read them. I suppose my being somewhat forced to finally write one at that point was karma.

But I wanted this blog about cancer to be different. I didn't want it to be merely facts and I didn't want it to be depressing. I wanted it to be funny. Plus I needed B to know that I had miraculously turned happy and was hopeful that he'd care enough at some point to want to talk to me. I set out to do an introduction to "The Humorous Life."
www.caringbridge.org/visit/tiffanyallen.

But I had a few doubts about venturing into the blog-o-sphere. Will anyone even read it, and more importantly, will they think it's funny? I considered that maybe I should get one of my funnier siblings to ghostwrite for me. I also wanted people to know individually how much I loved and appreciated them but wasn't sure how to communicate that in a blog post. Lastly, I had a ton of anxiety about making my blog super awesome, or at least not screwing it up. If I screwed up my blog, it was like I screwed up cancer. Yes, I was actually worried that I could screw up cancer. After all, I was on a mission to prove that I could change and that I could find happiness all by myself; therefore, I had to ROCK this cancer thing!

Despite my fears, the Humorous Life gave me an outlet. I was able to share my journey and the difficulty that went with it. But because I had named it The Humorous Life, I always tried to put on my humor glasses before posting. It kept me from wallowing in self-pity and at the same time I got feedback and support through others' comments and replies. The Humorous Life made it okay to share my fears while still looking for the silver lining, which was helpful because it wasn't just baldness that terrified me.

Right up there with my fear of baldness is my fear of needles. When I say I'm afraid of needles, I don't just mean I get a little queasy when I get a flu shot. I mean I am terrified of them. This was highlighted many times in my life (including fainting after getting my ears pierced), but one of my favorites was in college when I was late for class. I took a shortcut through the large student center where they were having a blood drive. As I raced through the corridor, staring at the ground to make sure I had no chance of catching even a peripheral glimpse of the lawn chair looking things that had all those people with needles the size of straws in their arms, I was only halfway through when I started to feel that rare but unmistakable feeling. My eyesight started to blur, sounds started to get muffled, my head started to spin, and my legs got wobbly. I knew what was next. I slumped down on a bench still 30 feet or so from the blood sucking, and I was out cold. The next thing I remember was some nice lady shaking me gently. When I could get my eyes to open, she was standing there with some juice and said smiling, "Did somebody try to get up and leave too soon?" Imagine my embarrassment when I had to tell her that I didn't give blood. I was just passing through on my way to class.

Later in my college career, I was asked by a roommate to come and be her moral support during a nerve conduction test that would involve the doctor sticking needles in various locations from her hand all the way to her shoulder. Years had passed since the blood drive so I thought maybe I had matured out of my fears. I stood bravely beside her as the doctor started from her hand and slowly made his way up to her shoulder. Somewhere near the insertion of the very last needle, I felt the room start to spin, my lips became tingly, and the voices around me became muffled. I slid down the wall and slumped to the floor. The doctor immediately stopped what he was doing and came to attend to me. I could hear him but couldn't get my eyes to open or any part of my body to respond. Seeing as I was taking first aid at the time, I do remember being impressed as I lay there that he was following the exact steps I had just learned for when you come across an unconscious victim. Although unable to move or respond, I distinctly remember having the thought, "Hey, I'm the unconscious victim!" Weird. The down side was that in his haste to help me, he had left the needle stuck in my roommate's arm. "Needle-less" to say (I know, bad joke), I was never asked to be moral support again.

To even better explain how monumental and ingrained my fear was, I should probably share one last story. Having been taught at a young age that God answers prayers, my best friend and I decided when we were little girls to start praying every day that there would be an epidural in pill form before we were old enough to have babies, because we both knew we would literally never survive having someone put a needle in our spine. (I suppose at this point, I've effectively driven home the fact that I was a neurotic child. On a side note, that friend now has 5 kids, and though we no longer keep in touch, rumor has it she survived.) So when I say I'm afraid of needles, I'm not being dramatic.

Besides the baldness, the other thing I knew about chemo was that it involved needles. The surgeon talked to me about the option of having a "port" as an alternative to getting an IV at every treatment. From the minute he told me what a port was and that it would be surgically implanted just below my clavicle, I told him to never say that word again. He actually took to whispering it from that point on. After a few more crying fits (sprinklings in comparison to the cloudbursts surrounding the chemo decision but still fairly flood-worthy), I agreed to the port. Pepe le Port (as I took to calling him) stayed hidden under bandages until the last second before my first chemo treatment. I couldn't look at him or touch him and tried my best to not even let my mind acknowledge his existence.

Over the first few weeks, I pondered my budding relationship with Pepe. He was definitely my Mr. Right Now. Even with his redeeming qualities, I gave us six months tops. Yet another relationship that wouldn't go the distance but at least this time, I'd be the one ready to move on. In the end, my love affair with Pepe was more love than hate. I eventually could look at him and even touch him and while he was still a large unmistakable and ugly protrusion from my chest, he provided both quick and fail-proof access to my veins. With a dollop of Lidocaine cream and some Ativan, I could almost forget what was happening. Almost.

I started chemo treatment with Adriamycin, nicknamed Red Devil or Big Red. Adriamycin was the big gun. I didn't fully understand the nickname until the first time I watched it run through the tubing into Pepe. It was not only dark red, but it turned my urine red. One of the scariest realizations of what I was doing to my body came during my first treatment when the nurse came in to administer the drug dressed in something resembling a hazmat suit. Seeing her enter the room basically covered from head to toe to avoid any contact with this substance that would soon be dripping into my body was unnerving. That fear was only exacerbated when I wheeled my IV pole into the restroom (Big Red seemed to flush right through me) and found hazardous material warning signs posted in there as well. Apparently it was just as toxic coming out as it was going in.

Lesson Learning: You never know how strong you are until being strong is the only choice you have.

The oncology nurse had told me that I would most likely lose my hair around the second dose of Big Red. With that knowledge, I had applied for financial assistance from a local nonprofit to get my parents there for that treatment. It was the one part of the journey I knew I couldn't do alone. I woke up the morning of my second date with Pepe feeling pretty confident that I had beaten the odds with the whole hair loss thing. I was so happy to have my parents there to support Pepe and me but was feeling a little guilty that I had gone to such lengths to get them there when it appeared my hair might remain intact.

I spent the morning lying on the couch, chatting with them about who knows what, until it was just about time for me to take a shower. I turned my head to look at the clock and felt something very strange. The back of my head that was against the armrest was aching. The actual scalp felt like it was burning. And then it hit me. I had read that one little-known part of cancer is that it's painful to lose your hair. That's one of the reasons I had determined I would cut my hair short to avoid both the trauma of the giant long globs of hair falling out, and to minimize the weight pulling on my hair follicles as the poor things took their beating. Apparently I didn't go short enough. My scalp seemed angry. I wasn't sure exactly how the whole process of hair loss worked. The pain was a circle on the back of my head. Was I just going to lose that patch like a newborn baby that sleeps on its back and gets that funky bald spot?

I told my parents about my scalp and then got in the shower. As soon as I started to wet down my hair, I could feel it. As I ran my fingers through my hair, I felt it begin to tangle around each finger. It was coming out everywhere. I did the only thing I could think of at that moment. In a slightly quivering voice, I called

"Mom?" Then she was there and as my eyes burned with tears, I stuck my hair-filled hands out of the shower curtain. As she began to reassure me, she carefully pulled all the hair from my fingers. She stayed in the bathroom as I continued to wash and gather my hair. The bathtub started to quickly fill up with soapy water as my drain became completely filled with what I had not been able to catch.

To my utter surprise though, the tears were brief. By the time I got out of the shower, I was sure I was ready for this next stage. I could do this. I was ready to lose my hair.

I started blow drying what was left on my head and ended up with a sink full of even more hair. My sweet mom, who had complained during my entire adolescence about the hair I left all over the house, wiped every bit of that hair up. We headed off for treatment and by the end of the day, I realized something odd. The day had gone fabulously. My dad watched each process, fascinated, and wanting to know every step that his little girl would be going through. My mom did exactly as she was told and hid her eyes from the needles. (It's never been any surprise where my needle phobia came from.) But Mom did great, I did great, and rather than going back to work after treatment as I normally would, I took the rest of the day off.

I wasn't so naive as to think that I was just going to sail through the whole bald thing based on that first day, but although my hair was giving up the ghost, just for that day I had set my biggest fear on the shelf. I was able to cheerfully introduce my parents to my fellow Friday chemo cronies, all of us with needles in ports or in arms, each of us fully aware that we were sending a type of poison into our veins that we all hoped would save our lives. Feeling brave with my parents there (and the help of the Ativan), I even watched the fluids drip into Pepe that day. I actually kept my eyes open while Pepe forked out some blood for a blood draw and when he got a nice saline bath to make sure he was all clean for our next date.

If you would have told that little girl who prayed for a needle-free epidural that her future held the choice to hang out with Pepe for six months or receive weekly IVs and blood draws, I'm sure you would have witnessed a resounding panic attack. I was still that scared little girl, but I made a choice and there was no going back. A friend sent me a text during treatment that said, "You never know how strong you are until being strong is the only choice you have." Truer words were never spoken. That little adage, the myriad of cards that had begun to pour in, the comments on my blog posts, and the simple reminders of support seemed to result in these bursts of strength and bravery. Days like those had to be soaked up because the roller coaster ride of cancer is unpredictable, a lot like the roller coaster of divorce . . . and the roller coaster of life.

Chapter 17:
Roses & Thorns

Sometimes good things fall apart so better things can fall together.—Marilyn Monroe

While I was going through treatment, my mom was assigned to teach a Sunday school class of nine-year-olds. Each Sunday, in addition to praying for me, they would review their "Roses & Thorns" for the week. Cancer was full of roses and thorns. Most of the thorns are probably obvious so let me share a few roses.

- I never threw up, not one time! The concoction of meds that Doc Ganales had me take before and after each chemo treatment was a work of brilliance.

- Decadron is an amazing drug that can have you bouncing off walls at 3 a.m. I found myself doing the most odd things in the middle of the night on this drug, such as going through every pen in my house to see which ones still wrote, zip tying every bundle of cords I could find on everything electronic within reach (and some that were not so easy to reach), and sorting/re-sorting every piece of paper within view. It was more than I'd gotten done around the house in probably—oh, I don't know—forever.

- Because I was "battling" cancer, in essence, I was able to take a break from battling divorce. The thorn of that rose is that I picked up right where I had left off when the cancer battle was over and my already slow progress was then 18 months behind schedule. But still, cancer was a distraction of sorts and I felt that with cancer, unlike with divorce, I was fighting a battle I could win.

- One day during treatment, I realized I wasn't interested in reading an article I saw on depression. This was a huge moment. I had always clung to everything I could get my hands on about anxiety and depression. Throughout my entire life, I had to click on every link, read every article, and buy every book about these issues that seemed to make up my very existence. But during cancer, surprisingly my depression and anxiety took a little break. Was it because I had another battle to focus on? Possibly. Or maybe it was all the drugs. Who knows? But I couldn't remember a time when I had ever glossed over anything on depression and when I realized that I had, I was pretty ecstatic.

- When you lose your hair (and no one really seems to talk about this), you lose *all* of your hair. While the ones on your head are particularly missed, the ones on your legs, underarms, and various other parts of your body that require hair maintenance are not missed one bit. I had many glorious months of two-minute showers that, in addition to requiring no conditioner and shampoo, required no shaving! Hea . . . ven!

Lesson Learning: There are always roses among the thorns. Love the roses for their beauty and the thorns for making you strong.

Chemo and radiation are certainly no fun. But I felt a little Herculean going through them. Oddly, my experience with both would be what I would rely on when the divorce demon returned. If I could be strong once, I could be strong again, couldn't I? But the first step was to own where I was on the path to recovery, even if the reality wasn't pretty. Cancer brought about its own kind of external ugly factor but that was just the beginning of the ugly I needed to face.

Chapter 18:
Owning My Ugly

My ability to turn good news into anxiety is rivaled only by my ability to turn anxiety into chin acne.
—Tina Fey

In the midst of chemo, my new tenants (four college students) informed me that they had a drippy faucet. I thought, well hey I can probably figure that out! It was a warm day and I didn't feel like wearing my wig but also didn't want to flaunt the bald head, so I put on a bandana. I took some channel locks and a few other tools and headed over. Trying my best to look like I knew what I was doing, I was under the sink loosening the cold water connection. One problem. Chemo brain makes one very forgetful. I had forgotten to turn off the water main first. Water exploded from the connection and blew the bandana right off of my little old man head. I tried to battle the pipe to get it reconnected but realized I was losing, so I screamed for the tenants to turn off the water main.

They were running around the house until, through the water spraying in my face as I kept trying to reattach the line, I yelled that it was outside. By the time they found it and all was said and done, I was soaked head to toe sitting in two inches of water with my head scarf floating nearby and the water flooding into the hallway carpet and nearest bedroom. All I could say as they came back to see me holding the channel locks, water dripping from my sparse hair and lashless eyelids was, "Well, I guess the secret's out. I'm bald!"

After finishing chemo and before starting radiation, I went to visit my sister and her family. Up until that point, I had decided that I was going to let my hair do whatever it was going to do. I wasn't going to shave it. Instead, I was left with stragglers that were a few inches long and remained scattered around my head. I looked like Jeff Dunham's "Peanut" puppet. It was a horrible look. Given my propensity for regrets, I still kick myself for waiting until my sister finally convinced me that a nice zero shave was a good idea. I spent a lot of time looking ridiculous. I also regret not just Bic-ing my head while I had the chance. After all, it looked hot on Demi Moore's "G.I. Jane." Now I'll never know. The zero shave was definitely an improvement though, and God bless my sister for finding a nice way of convincing me to do it and my brother-in-law for sporting the zero shave with me.

Unfortunately the zero shave didn't happen until the last day of the trip and, in the end, it may have been the reaction of my young niece to my hideous look that prompted my sister to convince me to do it. Two things I love about kids—their complete honesty and their sweet compassion. Shayla, the third of my sister's four children, was a spunky five-year-old when I showed up in all my ugly. I love this kid, although I do not wish her teenage years on anyone. She's now eight, going on seventeen. My sister's in for a ride.

One day we made plans to go to the pool. I was excited because, after six months of having to stay out of the sun, I could finally soak it up. I still had to do it lathered in factor-30 sunscreen but that's par for the course when your skin is so pale you border on transparency. Nevertheless, I wanted to go soak up the sun, no wig, sparse random hair floating in the breeze. I had packed an incredibly old (nearly transparent itself) bathing suit with flowers on it that I'd had for years. My sister asked if I wanted to wear one of hers instead. I chose a cute tankini with a solid peach top and brown bottoms. Granted I looked horrid in peach but I looked horrid anyway, so no worries there.

All was well until Shayla saw that I was going to wear my sister's suit instead of my own. She had the most concerned look I think I've ever seen on such a young face. "Aunt T, you have to wear the one with flowers! You HAVE to! If you don't, everyone will think you're a boy!" She was so genuinely concerned and distressed, I did my best to hide my smile. I tried to explain to her that people would still know I was a girl even without my hair. But she was adamant. She didn't want anyone thinking I was a boy and in her young mind, a bathing suit with flowers was my only fighting chance. Throughout my entire bald era, Shayla was always the most concerned. My sister told me that she would ask regularly if my hair was growing back yet and how long it was. Apparently being a boy is a fate worse than death when you're a five-year-old girl.

Make no mistake though, Shayla is not 100% compassion. During that same trip, I laid down with her one day for nap time. We were facing each other on the bed and she had her eyes closed. I was just watching her when suddenly her eyes flew open. After a few seconds, she looked slightly annoyed and slightly disturbed at the same time. I didn't think much about what I must look like lying there watching her with no eyelashes, no eyebrows, and only a few pieces of hair on my head. But it was all brought to my attention when she finally said, "Aunt T, stop looking at me with your freaky eyes!" Out of the mouth of babes.

I had to learn after a time to just own my ugly. Sure, I could don a wig, fake eyelashes, and some fake eyebrows, and I did. But there was a part of me that always felt like it was a bit of false advertising, something akin to a padded bra. After all, I really was bald. I really had no eyelashes and eyebrows. I really was sick. I've since met so many women who wore their baldness proudly and some who even chose to keep their hair short when it started to grow back. These women amaze me and I admire their confidence. While I'd like to say that I became completely self-confident after cancer, it's just not true. But what I realized is that we often receive an extra dose of strength during the thick of a battle. And regardless of how much we think we go back to "normal" or back to our old selves after the adrenaline rush of fighting a dragon, we are never the same. We cannot come out the same as we went in. It is neurobiologically impossible. We have forged a new pathway in our brain, a new coping skill, and if we allow ourselves to feel it and then resort to muscle memory so to speak, we can find a new little inkling of confidence. After all, even in the midst of believing it was not survivable, we found ourselves emerging on the other side.

Lesson Learning: Owning your ugly is the first step toward loving yourself.

Owning my ugly isn't just something I learned through cancer. It's hard to admit sometimes that we have ugly parts. Sure we love to talk about all the things that are wrong with us physically, but it's much harder to talk about our internal ugly. The fact is though, we all have it. There are a myriad of things I can't stand about myself. Some of them I was able to keep hidden for most of my life. Some of them were so blatantly obvious I had no choice but to fess up. Then there were those that I thought I kept hidden but found I was only fooling myself.

One example happened on a trip I took to Hawaii over my third and final wedding anniversary. The last of my college roommates was getting married. B didn't go with me. Later, evidence would surface that made it appear he had instead flown to Tucson and spent time with the woman he would leave me for less than 2 months later. But at that point, I was still completely oblivious to his discontent.

Most of my roommates had been married since college or soon after, so I had developed pretty good relationships with their spouses over many years. It was easy to be myself around them, although none of them knew me half as well as their wives did, or at least I had supposed that to be the case. We had spent the first day all together just hanging out bobbing around in the ocean and catching up. These were people who knew me well and whom I trusted. But apparently over the years, I had revealed a little too much information about myself and my weaknesses.

While the girls were doing our girly thing on the day of the wedding, the boys were out exploring the town. That night at the reception dinner we were able to all sit together. After the catching up was done, we were left with a whole night for fun. Being with them was always a complete blast, full of laughter, reminiscing, ribbing, etc. I was a little surprised however when the husbands told me they had all gone in and bought me a gift that day. One of them pulled out a package and handed it to me. As I curiously opened it, I couldn't help but be a little flattered that they had done something like this for me. After all, I was the only one there without my spouse, and although it was hard to feel like an extra wheel with this group, I was still wishing B was with me and that he was hanging out with the husbands. He was so easy to take places. He always fit right in.

I pulled out an odd-looking wooden statue about a foot tall with a face that looked like something you'd see on a totem pole. I'm sure I looked totally puzzled even while trying to look grateful. The husbands could hardly hold in their laughter. "Turn it over!" one of them finally said. On the bottom was the name of the statue: "God of money." Wow. I knew I had probably talked a lot about my feelings on money over the years and certainly about how our different financial views seemed to be such a huge part of the rift between B and me. I guess there was also that time I had been on a reality makeover show where the producers had named the episode "Tight Wad Tiffany," but was my obsession with money really that obvious? I figured I could do one of two things at that point: I could be hurt or I could own it. I laughed hysterically. Being discovered and realizing that what I thought was hidden was actually incredibly transparent was eye-opening and a good lesson in owning my ugly. If only that were the first and last time I had to face it.

From a young age, I always wanted to be everyone's favorite. I thought that my career aspirations to be a motivational speaker and write a book were just born from my desire to help other people, but as it turns out, another part of my ugly was the discovery that my wanting to help other people actually had little to do with other people. Deep down I didn't actually care about other people as much as I cared about how people saw me. It was an eye-opening experience to discover one day in one of my umpteen million counseling sessions that my big dreams and aspirations were all attempts to gain external validation. I used to always say when people asked why I wanted to be a motivational speaker that, in my opinion, being a motivational speaker was like being the flower delivery guy. Everyone loved the flower delivery guy. Even if you hate the person who sent you the flowers, no one hates the flower delivery guy. It's humanly impossible. Even "I'm sorry I screwed up" flowers are usually well received . . . at least from the delivery guy.

But if I were being honest with myself, my biggest desire in a speaking career was for people to notice me, think I'm awesome, and make me famous and rich, with the end result being me living happily ever after. I would live in a beautiful place and travel the world, making people feel better about themselves and believing I cared. Perfect! Forget the fact that I was an expert in nothing, had no gems of wisdom, no life experience to speak of, and became totally nervous at the idea of public speaking. All trivial matters. I was also completely ignoring the fact that I actually wanted to care, and my seeming inability to do so truly ate at me. Deep down I knew I could never be completely happy just pretending.

That day in counseling, realizing that all my dreams stemmed from a wish to validate myself through others because I lacked the ability to do it from within, was disturbing. Even more disturbing was the churning in my stomach as the insecurities bubbled from their kept-at-bay status to their front-and-center status. This whole self-love thing eluded me. I mean, I didn't hate myself so I always just assumed that meant I loved myself. Au contraire. Apparently not hating yourself does not automatically equate to loving yourself. Who knew? And what was I supposed to do with this knowledge? How do I make myself love myself? I can't even make myself get dressed some days!

But one thing I did realize was that this was a part of my ugly. So I owned it. I talked about it. I've now confessed it in a book! I hope that in the recognition and openness, I can begin to accept it. Make no mistake though, it's one of the many parts of me that still feels uncomfortably ugly.

Chapter 19:
Who am I Writing For?

Sometimes the thoughts in my head get so bored they go out for a stroll through my mouth. This is rarely a good thing.—Scott Westerfield

I'm not a writer. I'm a business analyst. A spreadsheet junkie. Trying to get this journey on paper has been excruciating at times. Just today I had a complete meltdown. I wasn't sure where to go next, what to write about, or how to put all my jumbled stories and memories into anything cohesive that another human being would want to read. It's days like this when I wonder what in the world I was thinking when I started this endeavor. Who am I to write a book? I'm a work in progress. I have no grand conclusions, no fairy tale ending. I haven't taken drastic measures to "find myself." I've just plugged along each day. Scratch that. I've plugged along many days. But some days I've crashed and burned. I've said it before; this journey isn't linear. In fact, I'd say it would make the most ridiculous and meaningless-looking graph if my analytic mind tried to plot it out. But I have to finish telling my story. I just have to. This is why.

I am the queen of starting things and not finishing them. I went to real estate school, even took the test, but never did one thing with it. I started my pilot's license and got a whopping 2 flight hours in my log book. Determined I was going to follow my dream to be a motivational speaker, I joined Toastmasters but only made it to speech #5 of 10. When asked if I would be the president of the club the following year, I immediately panicked and dropped out. I've tried to learn Spanish I don't know how many times. I have a nearly 30-year-old flute in a dusty case with a broken handle and a keyboard that hasn't had the cover off in months. I wanted to run a 5k, so I started following the Couch to 5k program, which gets you to a 5k in eight weeks. I quit on Day One of Week Eight. Even now, I'm not writing because I enjoy the process of writing a book. Honestly, I don't really want to write a book. I just want to have a book written that lists me as the author. How lazy is that? But unfortunately, the thing won't write itself. So I will keep on writing. I will finish something this time if only to prove to myself that I can.

Lesson Learning: Start for the wrong reasons if that's all you've got, but start.

In the beginning, this book was supposed to be an attempt to show B that he was wrong, to prove to anyone who read it that he made a mistake. I wanted to show that I had become this amazing rock star of a person and everyone, most especially him, would recognize his loss. Even if he didn't come running back to me, as long as he felt regret (and this of course had to be confirmed), then my mission would be accomplished. Crazy alert: some days "Operation: Get B to Regret" still clouds my writing. So rather than let it continue to darken my process, I'm going to just throw some light on it and air it out a bit.

Every day that I sit to write, I remind myself who I want to be writing for. I want to be writing for anyone else who might be struggling in their battle against depression, divorce, or cancer. I want to be writing for myself. I want to reach the girl who was me when my world first fell apart and there seemed to be no light ahead, and I want to give her hope.

I remind myself that it's a waste of time to write for B. It doesn't matter what he would think. Happily ensconced in a new and apparently easier life, my words would certainly give him no cause for regret, and ever since his departure, it appears he's not interested in whether or not I've survived the depression, the divorce, or even the cancer. His silence over the years has spoken volumes. Regardless of the truth about how he does or doesn't feel though, I cannot write for him. In telling my story however, I'm in part telling his. That causes some trepidation as there may be many who know the two of us who might either read or hear about this book, and I can't know for sure how it will be perceived. I want to tell my story from my perspective and share my process of working through it, but the people pleaser part of me worries that the perception of airing dirty laundry will be hurtful and ill received. That thought makes this an even more difficult process.

People pleasers don't want anyone to be mad at them, ever. That has always felt like a fate worse than death to me. But I suppose I also thought baldness was a fate worse than death, and I survived that. So do I care more about what other people think of me or more about the possibility that my honesty could be helpful to someone? Truthfully, the idea that anyone would be angry had not even occurred to me until recently. Why was that? Probably because it didn't fit in with my original grand plan. My honest book was going to soften hearts, help shed light on what I've been going through, and reveal how I've changed. There was no room in my vision for anger or any negative fallout. Only acceptance, love, and forgiveness. So either I have more optimism than I give myself credit for or more naiveté than I care to admit.

My story doesn't just involve what happened to me though; it also involves my reactions to those things, and my reactions on occasion have been less than sane. They may have even been a little crazy. But I want to be honest about those parts too. Do people write about this side of themselves? Do people admit they have crazy parts? It seems that cool people like Tina Fey and Mindy Kaling can admit they have some crazy, and everyone just thinks they're cooler for it. But for me to talk about my crazy means people will know (as if they didn't already suspect) just how crazy I can be sometimes. For all I know, my friends and even my family may think it best to take a few steps back after reading this. But maybe there's also someone who needs to know that there are others who have felt the same crazy, and that crazy doesn't mean hopeless.

I'm still fearful that anyone might get angry, but I try to quiet the voice that asks what "they" will think and just keep writing; and each day that I continue to write, I'm starting to notice subtle differences. Maybe I'm able to tell a story a bit more freely. Maybe I'm not even thinking about B when I write. Rather, I might instead find myself thinking about the girl who existed six months ago, two years ago, six years ago. What would she need me to say to her? What would she need to hear when she believed the pain was not survivable? If I hadn't started writing for the wrong reasons, I may have never started writing at all. But I feel in my gut that something is emerging from inside that is a whole lot healthier than what has been on the surface for so many years. So I keep writing, despite what the motivations may be. Movement in any direction is movement, and I'll take it.

Chapter 20:
The Ancient Shrink & Pale Girl

People will love you. People will hate you. And none of it will have anything to do with you.
—Abraham Hicks

One of the worst experiences can be feeling judged, and the feeling is only amplified in those of us with fragile self-images. If someone so much as looks at us the wrong way, we immediately create an entire story about how it must have been due to some stupid thing we said the other day, and that person must have told this person who then decided that we're now stupid in general and they're now going to tell all our friends about our stupidity, leaving us friendless . . . and stupid. I've always obsessed about the judgments I perceive others are placing on me, and I'm sure I'm not alone. But sometimes we just need to take those judgments (perceived or otherwise) with a grain of salt. Especially when we realize that oftentimes we can find ourselves on the distributing end just as easily as the receiving end.

Lesson Learning: Take judgments with a grain of salt and steer clear of doling them out.

Case in point. After B left, I continued to see the counselor that we had been seeing during our marriage. However, I needed to get a new psychiatrist for my prescriptions. Since I was now working for a hospital with its own outpatient mental health, I called and asked for a recommendation from the clinic staff. Without hesitation, they told me Dr. Z. I walked into Dr. Z's office and was greeted with the warmest and most gentle smile. But that didn't overcome my shock at the fact that this guy looked like he was in his 80s. As it turned out, he was 88. Dr. Z worked four full days a week. When I asked him once why he didn't retire, his response was, "Why would I? I love what I do!" I came to love Dr. Z but I would never have seen that coming from my first visit.

The initial evaluation visits are always longer (yes, I know that from years of experience) and they ask you everything about everything. I was incredibly uncomfortable talking to this old man about all the intimate details of my life and my craziness. I was certain that there was no way he could be of any help to me, a little miffed that the staff had recommended him, and somewhat disturbed that the hospital would even employ him. When I saw my counselor again after my initial visit with Dr. Z, I gave him an earful. Did he know much about the psych docs they had at the hospital? I told him I had asked for a recommendation and they sent me to an incredibly old man who probably shouldn't even still be working! How in the world could he even relate to me? I told the counselor about Dr. Z asking me about my sex life and talking about it with me at great lengths. I told him how incredibly uncomfortable I was and that it was like talking to my grandpa! Or to a dirty old man! My counselor smiled the entire time. When I finally paused to let him respond, his response stopped me dead in my tracks. "Yes, I know Dr. Z well. He's my father-in-law."

Gulp. Panic. Embarrassment. I completely backpedaled and started stumbling over my words. Dr. Z did seem very nice and genuine. He obviously loved what he did. He spent a lot of time with me. The staff obviously loved him because they recommended him, so I'm sure I was in the hands of the best. Blah blah blah. He continued to just smile. It was probably this faux pas that kept me going to Dr. Z, and as it turned out I began to enjoy our visits. He would always greet me with a huge smile. Then he would ever so slowly rise from his chair and give me a hug. He was always so genuinely interested in how I was doing and would even check on me between appointments. That said, I never stopped having the fear that I would walk into his office one day and he would greet me with that huge smile but he wouldn't rise from the chair. He would have died right there, with the warm smile on his face, doing what he loved. I saw Dr. Z until just before he finally sustained an injury that physically didn't allow him to come back to work. He was 91. Shooting my mouth off about Dr. Z was a reminder that not only can I easily find myself on the delivery side of judgment, but that I can also find my judgments to be dead wrong. This was an important lesson to remember when the tables were turned.

We've all been judged. Even during cancer, I somehow managed to find myself on the receiving end of judgment. As much as I loved Dr. Ganales, she had a way of pointing out my downfalls. For one, she was always asking about my dating life. Sure I could tell her about the guy I met online from Santa Cruz who let me pay for our meal, but who also, knowing I was going through chemo, brought me his last "bud" from his very own marijuana garden. I could tell her all kinds of stories but no matter what I told her, she always seemed to point out that I was somehow messing it up. "Stop telling them you have cancer!" she would say. Hard to do when during another attempt at a first date, I was asked out on a motorcycle ride. We stopped for him to take a phone call, and as I went to take off my helmet I realized it was too tight and if it came off, my wig would come off with it. I paced around for several minutes wearing that dumb helmet and then finally hid behind a sand dune to pull the whole mess off and get my hair back on. When the ride was over though, and it was time to take the helmet off for good, there was nowhere to hide. He never called again. I was okay with that.

Doc Ganales was relentless. On one appointment, she told me "You look really pale." The entire time I'd been sick, I'd had no small number of people tell me how pale I looked. I'm pretty pale normally. Overlooking the over-pigmentation on my face known as freckles and the fact that my hair isn't white and my eyes aren't pink, the rest of me looks very similar to an albino. I told her that since I'd been sick, a lot of people had been pointing out that I looked pale. "No, no!" she said in her thick Russian accent, "you need lipstick!" I suppose if you're in the middle of cancer treatment and your oncologist is concerned about your lack of lipstick, that's a pretty good sign that your prognosis is rosy.

But the skin color issue didn't end with the Doc. I'd made friends with the medical assistant who would take my vitals at each appointment. We would share some laughs and she'd try to console me as the scale continued to go up and up every time I weighed. Maricela would then give me a clipboard with a form to fill out, listing how I was feeling at that moment, what symptoms I'd had since my last appointment and anything I wanted to share with the doc or ask about. I usually filled this out with running commentary to bounce some things off of her and make sure I wasn't exaggerating or glossing over anything.

At one particular appointment, I remembered that I needed to tell the doc about a rash I'd developed. It had been there for a few weeks and I had failed to mention it at my last appointment. I pulled up my pant leg to show

Maricela. Bear in mind that when I showed my coworkers they said, "Oh my gosh, that looks bad! Does it itch? Does it hurt? You need to tell the doctor right away!" So I was expecting something along those lines. Instead, this is what I got . . . "Wow, girl! You need to get yourself a tan! You are SOOOO white!" Yes, I've heard that a lot in my life. Yes, I'd heard it even more while I was sick. But I had literally just returned from a family vacation to the beach and since I couldn't be in the sun during treatment and given that I'd be wearing a turban with no eyelashes, my parents wanted me to feel as good as I possibly could. The gift they gave was perfect and I had loved rocking it on the beach! But their gift made hearing about my paleness even more disturbing this time. I can't imagine what my face must have looked like as the shock came over it. I finally recovered enough to inform her about my gift. "I HAVE A SPRAY TAN!" The incredulity on her face at that point was priceless! Another good laugh.

My friends and medical team were absolutely right about my skin. For me to have been offended would have been silly. They weren't making judgments about my character, just my pigment. But I was truly judgmental about Dr.

Z. I knew absolutely nothing about him when I determined he would be of no use to me. My actions were no different than if someone would have judged me because they heard I was divorced . . . or depressed . . . or had cancer. There were plenty of other times when I was on the receiving end of hurtful suppositions, but it makes me feel powerful when I can see those judgments for what they are, of no consequence and frequently completely untrue. I look forward to the time when I'm able to give someone the benefit of the doubt when they're guilty of what I myself have stooped to. That's growth. That's progress. That's change. So I continue to try to take unfair judgments with a grain of salt and steer clear as much as possible of doling them out. We are products of our perceptions and sometimes there is no right or wrong; there is just someone's opinion. And if you think opinions can't change, look at what you thought was cool to wear 20 years ago. Just sayin'.

Chapter 21:
Mental Meltdown

She's crazy. And just when you think you've reached the bottom of her craziness, there's a crazy underground garage.
—Will Truman, "Will & Grace"

After divorce and cancer, one would have thought that I'd come out stronger. Or at least I thought I would. I'm sure I was stronger, but similar to the terrible choices I'd made in my marriage which led to its downfall, I was about to make another bad decision that would send me to the mat again.

I mentioned before that after my cancer treatment was over, it was almost like I had put mourning my divorce on hold, and somehow I picked up right where I had left off more than a year prior. Things in my life were settling back into normal, my hair was starting to grow back and the adrenaline that I'm pretty sure coursed through me while trying to show I could be brave during the entire cancer treatment process had drained from my system entirely. The loneliness was again palpable. The hurt of receiving no encouragement from B was suddenly a much heavier weight. I wasn't at the forefront of everyone's attention anymore. The insecurities that I managed to joke about and turn humorous during cancer now just seemed pathetic. I started to find myself getting more and more weepy, more and more sad. I had been on antidepressant drug number who-knows-what for quite some time at this point, and I blamed my sadness on the fact that it just must not be as effective anymore. And then I hit a wall. I got sick of taking so many medications. So one day, I just stopped taking them. I had been on medications off and on for almost 20 years and I felt like I was still suffering. I figured I must not need them anyway since they weren't doing much good. Or so I thought.

About a week later, I was in an exercise class and got so dizzy that I had to crawl out of the gym and lie on the hallway floor. It took almost an hour before I could even sit up and eventually get to my car. I had no clue what was going on until someone asked me if I'd changed any medications lately. In my brainiac move, I had apparently taken myself off the antidepressant that is known for having the very worst withdrawal symptoms. I realized I was detoxing, and it was hell. My sleep became erratic and I had some weird tinny sound in my ears. Things just spiraled down until, after several weeks, I knew I was in trouble. I finally told my psychiatrist what I had done. We tried several new medication combinations, but I was in really bad shape. The decision was finally made to pull me out of work again. I tried just taking some time off. I even went to a four-day meditation retreat at a Tibetan Buddhist institute in Berkeley. But there seemed to be no stopping the train at that point and eventually, I was evaluated and placed in the Partial Hospital Program (PHP) at the hospital where I worked.

You really have to put all pride aside when the people you work with see you smack dab in the middle of your crazy. I was now being treated by people with whom I had interacted professionally. I had previously provided data and analysis for them and now I was their patient. I probably wasn't the first fellow employee to come through the program, but I felt like I was. And I was now spending five days a week, six hours a day in group therapy for a mental breakdown. I can't lie. It was humiliating and is still hard to talk about around most people without feeling a little judged. Unfortunately, mental health issues have a stigma. To hide my embarrassment, I had to make light of it. I joked that I was in the loony bin. And although I didn't feel like I was half as crazy as some of the people I met, and I certainly had the least dysfunctional childhood of all of them, there was a camaraderie shared in our vulnerability. There is a comfort in being able to say the crazy things on your mind and have others just nod their heads in understanding. I was desperate to find some kind of peace, any kind of relief from the dark place I had sent myself. These people became a safety net of sorts.

I spent six weeks in the program. I started back on medication. I was so desperate to feel better that I put myself on this intensely rigid schedule of prayer, meditation, diet, exercise, and sleep. I am task-oriented. I figured complete devotion to a rigid schedule would save me. The truth is, I hate being tied to a regimen but am completely terrified when I'm not. When a wide-open day is left up to me, I find myself panicking with how to fill it in the "best" way. I'm not sure how the "best" way is even determined, but without a rigid plan for my day, I would agonize over choosing the seemingly wrong things to fill my time.

I learned pretty quickly in the program that I could not hide from the fact that I was there. I was that person. I had melted down to the point that I was unable to function without getting serious help, and no one wants the "crazy" girl. I even saw a post on a dating website once that said you could contact him only if you were not, nor ever had been, on antidepressant medications. We are such judgmental creatures.

Despite the embarrassment of it all, I learned quite a bit in that program. For one, I learned that this kind of mental breakdown was no respecter of persons. On my third day or so, one of the most beautiful, chic, sophisticated women I had ever met started the program. She had actually just been released as an inpatient from the psych ward. I'll admit, I was totally floored that someone of her caliber would end up in the nut house. She had become suicidal and her (incredibly handsome and rich) husband had taken her to the hospital. She spent almost a week there before joining us. What I liked best about her, besides the myriad of amazing ensembles she wore, was that she owned what happened to her. She did not seem embarrassed. She only cared about learning to feel better. I was inspired.

Another important lesson I learned was that we stay in certain behavior patterns because we are gaining something from them. When I first started seeing my counselor, she asked me who I would be without my misery. I remember tearing up because I didn't know the answer. I had known misery for so long that I honestly couldn't see anything else out in front of me. If it were taken away I truly didn't know what would be left. That was a glaring indication that I might be hanging onto my victim mentality and all that went with it.

Lesson Learning: What I gain by remaining broken is far outweighed by what I gain by moving forward.

One thing about being in a full-time mental health program is that there is a lot of self-analysis and a lot of time to think. During one session, the conversation revolved around looking at what we were gaining by remaining status quo. I was somewhat appalled that anyone would assume that I actually chose suffering as my persona, so at first I was a little resistant to even participate. However, one thing I had decided going in was that I would do whatever was asked of me. After all, being left to my own devices obviously hadn't worked, so I promised myself I would listen to the experts and follow instructions.

When I really started to think about it, amazingly I saw what scared me about not being a depressed, anxious, and sad victim. For one, I could use it as an excuse not to participate in a lot of social activities that intimidated me. I didn't have to try and meet someone or seriously date because I was broken. I didn't have to do things for others, volunteer, serve, or look outside myself at all because I was broken. I could stay unhappy in my current circumstances and not try to change anything because, poor me, I was broken. I even discovered that I believed my illness gave my mom purpose. I knew it was hard for her not to be "mom" anymore to her grown kids, and with me in this condition, she was desperately needed. I was challenged at one point to have a conversation with her about this. I was really nervous because I had no idea how she would respond. But her response was beautiful and perfect. She told me that she realized she had been a helicopter mom and that the result had been, at least in my case, a grown-up who had trouble making her own decisions. She was right. I struggled with even the smallest decisions and always needed someone else's confirming opinion. Have my dad tell you sometime about dress shopping with me. Greater love hath no father.

Having recognized as I got older that while trying to protect me as a child may have actually hindered me, my mom wanted nothing more than to feel that I could function without her. I thought she would be sad if she wasn't hearing from me every day but she explained that how often we talked did not directly correlate with how much she thought I loved her. If my mom didn't need me to need her, another excuse to remain in my sad state would be eliminated.

Doing the work to become emotionally healthy also seemed hard. Too hard. I want the sure thing. I want to know that 15 minutes of meditation will automatically buy me 30 minutes of happiness, that if I write down three things I'm grateful for every day for three weeks, I'll become a full-blown optimist. I want to check things off my list every day and see tangible results directly related to my efforts. But this emotional health stuff is all intangible and fluffy. It certainly doesn't happen overnight and, oftentimes, like the healing of a broken heart, the change is not visible until we look back on what constitutes our painstaking efforts. This irritates me to no end and becomes my excuse to not even try.

While I've never had a huge struggle with weight, there have been times in my life (including the present) when I have been less than happy with the scale and wanted to lose weight. I would never diet though, and I am not a huge fan of exercise, so I wouldn't do much of that either. My reasoning was always that, if I never tried it, then I'd know it was always out there as an option. But if I tried it and it didn't work, the failure and disappointment would be so great that I couldn't handle it. In essence, diet and exercise were my last resort and I didn't want to face that my last resort may not work. So instead, I'd whine and complain about how awful I felt and then wait for some sort of event that would result in an involuntary weight loss. When I gained the freshman 20, I got my wisdom teeth out and ended up with horrible dry socket. I couldn't eat solid food for weeks. When I plumped up in grad school, I took a softball to the face and broke my nose. After a deviated septum repair, complete with tonsils and adenoids removed, I literally thought I would die for weeks. Weight gone again. And when I hit pretty much my highest weight ever during my marriage, well, the divorce diet was by far the quickest and most effective. But as with any other diet, it's not successful if you don't keep it off, and I subsequently gained back every pound.

Realizing there were actually reasons that I was choosing not to face my issues was both frustrating and scary, but it made me have to own my emotional health in a way I'd never had to before. There were things I was gaining by not becoming emotionally stronger. But there was plenty I was losing. The next important question to ask was if the benefits of staying the same outweighed the benefits of change and, maybe even more so, did the pain I was in outweigh the fear of moving forward. Moving forward was definitely not without pain, especially because I wasn't the only one who was affected by my state of mind.

Prior to going into PHP, I had shared an office with my coworker for several years. While I was in the program, our department moved to a new location. It had been the plan for her and me to continue to share office space, but just before I was about to complete the program, she sent an email saying that she and my boss had decided it would be best if we no longer shared space. I was given the choice of a cubicle or an office with no windows that was the furthest available space away from the main entrance. I was crushed, but I also understood. She had gone through a lot, having to be in the same room with my crazy mood swings, and she had to protect her own mental health. This was my first big challenge using the skills I had been learning. And while I had a myriad of emotions, I was able to respond in a way that didn't escalate the situation and hopefully showed that I understood. While I might have sworn back then that not much had changed when I left the program, taking the time to look back now, there's no question that there was progress. I didn't realize it at the time, but my response to being moved to a different office was progress. Though still a rocky road ahead, there would be even more progress in my future.

Chapter 22:
Smelling Frosting

Loving someone who doesn't love you back is like hugging a cactus; the tighter you hold on to it, the more it hurts.—Unknown

Music is powerful. Emotions bubble to the surface. Memories flood the mind. You can be instantly transported back to a time and a place that may have seemed completely gone and buried. After B left, there were a million songs that got to me. Of course, after making CDs for each other for so long, each of those songs had meaning. But there were other songs. Songs with lyrics like "When a heart breaks it don't break even," "I can't make you love me," "Tonight I wanna cry," and "Now you're just somebody that I used to know." Even after years of him being gone, "Say something, I'm giving up on you" still burns my eyes, lumps up my throat, and squeezes my chest. The happy songs got to me, the sad songs got to me. They were all filled with things I wanted to say, things I wanted him to say, all the reasons why he should come back, and all the reasons why he wasn't coming back.

But music isn't the only thing that can conjure emotion. When I was a baby, my parents owned a bakery. It was a very difficult and stressful time for them with a newborn and the demands of running a business. Sugar also took an unexpected and incredible leap in price during that time. Years later, my mom explained that because of the extreme difficulties of that period, the smell of frosting now would literally make her nauseous. The smell would transport her back to those days and she would get physically sick. We grew up with a saying in our family when something would happen that would bring up a negative physical or emotional response. "It's like smelling frosting."

As the years have passed and my emotions have been maybe not less raw but less able to overtake me for long periods of time, I wondered why B was never curious about how I was doing. He eventually cut off all communication and connection, even asking his mom not to talk to me. I remember asking a mutual friend once if he ever asked how I was doing. "Nope, not once," was the response. I truly didn't understand how you go from loving another person and committing to forever to literally not caring what happens to them. Sure you "hope for the best" for them, but how can you have no interest in knowing even the tiniest detail about their life? I still don't understand that. I'm told it's the way men deal with things. They compartmentalize. They shut it off, pretend it never happened, move on. But women, we're a different story. We may have compartments in our brain, but they're all open simultaneously and thoughts are jumping from one to the next. Rather than pretend it never happened, we agonize about how we could have changed it. We hold secret hopes that someday we'll get the chance to have a do-over.

Lesson Learning: Sometimes you smell frosting; sometimes you're the frosting that others smell.

In pouring my soul out to my mom one night and telling her how I didn't understand how he could have become indifferent and not even make any efforts to check on me or my well-being, she said it. "It's like smelling frosting for him. And once it's like smelling frosting, there's never any changing it. Never." Already in tears, I began to sob, repeating over and over, "I don't want to be B's frosting!" "There's nothing you can do about it," she said. That stupid darkness crept in again, the insecurity, the near crazy desire to do anything I could to make him see that I wasn't frosting! But the truth is, Mom was right. I am frosting to B. I will most likely always be his frosting, which is why I will most likely never see him again. Even now, that thought presses on me. "Why try to hold on so tightly to someone who let you go?" the critic voice says. I'm sure he "hopes for the best" for me. But I'd rather have him hate my guts. I'd rather have him be nervous at the thought of seeing me because of what he might feel and what he might have to face. Even negative emotion seems better than indifference. He slipped out of one life and into the next. I hit the rock bottom of loneliness, self-loathing, and despair. And now I was his frosting. I was the thought he no longer had or if he did, would shove it aside just as quickly as it came to avoid the nausea of the frosting smell.

I knew that nausea. When B left, I had a subliminal message cassette tape with positive affirmations that I listened to incessantly. I'm not exaggerating. I had it on night and day. I went to sleep with it on and I listened to it at work. I was so desperate. I did this for months. Years later, I pulled that tape out and put it on. Immediately, I thought I would be sick. The music took me straight back to those horrible days. It had become frosting. It went straight in the trash. Bye-bye tape.

But my frosting smells went much deeper than a subliminal message tape. And thinking of being B's frosting reminded me of Justin. After our broken engagement, Justin never really recovered. When he heard I was divorced, even after years of not really communicating, he asked to see me. "If we could just see each other, maybe you would feel something." I could hear the desperation and hope in his voice. But I knew there was no hope. I had no feelings for him anymore. No physical interaction would change that. I "wanted the best" for him. But I didn't want to give him false hope when there was none. I can hardly think about that situation now without the overwhelming realization that I'm B's Justin. I've spent many a night crying over the fact that I know just how B feels about me because it's how I feel about Justin. And I feel sorry for Justin. A random thought about him may cross my mind from time to time, but it rarely conjures up desire for contact. I am B's Justin.

After someone promises you forever, knows your deepest vulnerabilities, and then leaves you, especially for someone else, trust flies out the window. The belief that vows and covenants mean anything is completely destroyed. I found myself looking at couples and wondering if they were going to make it. Had they seen the other's ugly side yet? Would they stand by even in times of complete darkness and no hope? When they said, "For better or for worse," did they mean it? When they really got to worse, would they stay? Or would they "lose hope" and decide it was just too hard. To B, our marriage wasn't worth fighting for. I wasn't worth fighting for. How do you then go on to convince yourself otherwise? How do you make yourself believe that you're still worth fighting for after the very person who promised to fight for you decides you're no longer worth it?

I certainly haven't figured it all out, but I've figured out enough to know that only my own belief that I am worth the fight matters. I may be alone for the rest of my life. I can't afford to carry others' beliefs about me, especially the negative ones. But even the positive ones are not to hang my hat on. My hat needs to hang on a "screw what anyone else thinks; I'm awesome and totally worth fighting for" mentality. But to quote more song lyrics, "How do I get there from here?"

I have created my own frosting and have spent way too much time forcing myself to smell it. In the end, I hope that Mom is wrong about the whole frosting thing and that not only will the frosting smell fade for B, but that I can eventually walk into the bakeries of my life and not even notice the smell. The problem is, I keep deciding when I think that time should be, so I stick my nose in the wrong bakeries all the time. The Facebook bakery. The mutual friends' bakery. The looking-at-my-wedding-ring bakery. Thankfully (I think?), our wedding video also somehow escaped the "sentimental" box. When I stick my nose in that bakery, I wish I'd had the strength to toss it into the dark Mediterranean Sea with Surfer Ken, but I'm baby stepping. Maybe someday, the time will come for the departure of these remaining hold outs. But that's a dilemma for another day. In my quest to discover I'm worth fighting for, I had to start by facing some of the heaviest baggage on the road to recovery. If successfully ditched, however, it had the potential to yield far better results than chucking a little DVD.

Chapter 23:
Soberanes

When one has a famishing thirst for happiness, one is apt to gulp down diversions wherever they are offered.—**Alice Caldwell Rice**

It seemed to me that there was some sort of expectation out there that getting past divorce should take about six months. I have no idea where this magic number came from or if I somehow just created it in my own mind, but not only has it taken much longer than six months, I still find myself making some of the same mistakes and slipping into old patterns of thinking and acting. Don't feel discouraged by this. Instead feel encouraged that in spite of the backsliding and frustrations about slow progress, the overall post-divorce trajectory is forward, though like the stock market, full of ups and downs.

Almost a year after B left, I went to a holiday party at my neighbor's house. I noticed a tall, attractive guy with dreadlocks and tattoos. Not my normal type but he seemed friendly and funny. I realized that we worked for the same organization. I knew his name, so I got brave, approached him and asked, "Are you Soberanes?" I would later learn that the immediate look of suspicion he gave me was just part of his nature. We talked the night away with another fellow employee and then he offered to walk me home. I told him I literally lived right across the street. But he insisted. It seemed like a sweet, albeit unnecessary, gesture. We became fast friends, then we became more. I was grateful to have the attention, but we both knew that our lifestyles were too different to ever make a real go of anything. It seemed that being myself hadn't served me well in my marriage, so I threw myself into a situation where I thought if I could change and adapt enough, I could make it work. I tried to be more like him, tried to like the things he liked, tried to be what I thought he wanted me to be.

But this wasn't a regular relationship to begin with. Because he saw no future, it was never a relationship in his mind. No matter the level of intimacy, we were just good friends. I fought against this like nobody's business. I knew deep down he must feel something he wasn't telling me. No matter how many times he was brutally honest with me that he would only ever consider me a good friend, I threw myself into trying to prove him wrong. But I knew that, even as we spent time together, he was always open to the possibility of meeting someone else. So I asked him to please tell me if he ever met someone in whom he became interested. I didn't want to be played the fool again.

This lasted for a few years until finally he was done for good. No matter how honest he had been with me over the years, I was crushed. But even more painful was when he started a relationship just a few weeks later. Unbeknownst to me, he had met a girl six months prior. To make matters worse, she was a tall blonde, blue-eyed, gym/yoga lover who helped old people for a living. A beautiful, athletic saint. No way could I compete with that.

I was thrown immediately back into the "I'm not pretty enough, athletic enough, whatever enough" mindset. Yet again, I'm not the right fit for someone. Well then, whose fit am I? And because he hadn't told me about her I, in my mind, had been dumped yet again after someone else had been groomed in the background. I fell right back into my crazy. I kept trying to work through it by having continuous conversations with him in which he would remain stoic and tell me he was moving on and I needed to do the same, but that I would always be one of his best friends. I would be crying, angry, hurt, and sad. I don't know what I was looking for in those conversations, but whatever it was, I wasn't getting it. What I was getting was the same brutal reality that I had been fighting against with B. This was never going to be a good fit. I just wanted it to be. I was sure I could make it be. But instead, I was now watching Soberanes go through his new relationship phase. No matter how many people told me I was nuts for trying to remain his friend, it was important for me to prove to myself that I could do it.

I was frustrated. Why was I falling into the same trap? But recognizing what was happening this time, I tried to do things a little differently. Realizing that I wasn't in a good place emotionally, I backed out of an already planned trip to spend a holiday with his family. That was such a hard decision because I wanted more than anything to have that time with him, to have that time with his family, to solidify my place in his life. But after sound parental advice, I realized that going with him would put me in a situation where I would be forcing myself into an unnecessary and dangerously vulnerable position, where I would have nowhere to go to escape if I felt a meltdown coming, and where the huge possibility existed that I would do real damage to our chance at friendship.

Yes, maybe I was crazy for trying to maintain the friendship. But after losing B entirely, I suppose I was looking at this as my chance to behave differently. I never regretted my decision to stay home. For once, I didn't try to force myself to have something painful in my face to see if I could handle it. For once, I let it be okay to admit that I wasn't ready.

I learned another difficult lesson through that process. When it happened, I immediately let myself compare it to the pain I experienced with B. I let myself roll around in it, and wallow in the fact that this always happens to me and I'm never good enough. I'm always the one left alone while the other person walks right into another relationship. It happened with Jason, it happened with B, now it was happening again.

Lesson Learning: Everyone heals at their own pace; don't let anyone tell you yours.

But my wise counselor pointed out that I was at a crossroads. I could go down the path of bringing up all the old stuff or I could stop myself. I could beat myself up that it was taking so long to heal, or I could own the fact that everyone heals at their own pace. No one can tell me how long it should take and I should never let them. That doesn't mean that nothing is changing. It's okay to mourn the facts. Fact: I'm sad that our relationship in whatever form it was, ended. Fact: It hurts that he's with someone else. But that's where I need to stop myself. I need to stop saying that this means I'm not good enough. I need to stop conjuring up old hurts to justify that I'll never be good enough. I am good enough. I'm valued at my job. Good enough. I'm loved by my family. Good enough. Soberanes wanted me to have a place to go for the holidays. Good enough. I'm working hard to heal from B, and even though the pace is slow, and even though I fall into the same traps again and again, there are glimmers of hope. There are traces of light. For today, good enough.

Soberanes is now in a different relationship with a woman who seems an absolutely perfect match for him. I thoroughly enjoy their company and he and I have stayed wonderful friends (which, in case you're wondering, is why I allowed him to pick his own pseudonym.) My jealousy is gone. It's been replaced with happiness that someone I care deeply about found someone wonderful. I'm also choosing to look to his experience as one that gives me hope that the same thing may be out there for me somewhere. Maybe I'm changing after all. Good enough.

Chapter 24:
Sonya

You never need to apologize for how you choose to survive.—**Unknown**

As I approached and surpassed that magic six-month mark, and as a chronic over-sharer, I began beating myself up more and more for not minimizing my pain to those around me. It seemed there was some badge of honor to be earned for being tough and getting through divorce and cancer. Moving forward and forgiving and healing as fast as possible were praiseworthy. Well, of course I wanted to do all those things as fast as possible! But my fast as possible just wasn't very fast. I was never sure if I should pretend like I was sailing along and things were fine, or if I should be honest about how I really felt. I tried to remind myself of the fact that when most people ask, "How are you?" they don't necessarily really want to hear a long explanation of how you actually are. Even those who love you most don't necessarily want to hear you rehash the same stuff over and over. I really wanted to look tough, but I also didn't want to act like nothing was wrong when I still felt inside like everything was wrong.

With cancer, from the date of your diagnosis, you're considered a "survivor" until you leave this earth. Once I was a survivor of cancer, had completed my treatment and felt like life was getting back to some sort of normalcy, I wanted to focus on becoming a survivor of divorce. I thought the only way to do that would be to stop hurting, to not have my stomach do flip flops at the sound of his name, and to be able to say out loud (and mean it) that I was happy for his happiness. I knew I was nowhere near any of that being a reality, so I thought instead that I just needed to downplay my pain.

Lesson Learning: You don't need to minimize your heartbreak to be a survivor.

During cancer treatment, I met a beautiful, vibrant girl named Sonya. She was a few years younger than me and always came to the infusion center looking like a million bucks. I watched Sonya live her life even as she fought for it. She was a wife, a daughter, a sister, an aunt, a friend, and a coworker. She was beloved. Even as she was wheeled in for one of her final surgeries, she told her mom, "I want to live!" And she did. She lived up until the day she died. She was a survivor. But her survival was rocky and painful. It was full of a myriad of treatments, physical and emotional ups and downs, and faith-shaking moments. Despite her belief in heaven, she was heartbroken at the thought of leaving her sweet husband and family. Those who loved her knew her heartbreak. She didn't minimize it. Even through that heartbreak, through the pain, through the unknown, she was one of the best survivors I ever knew.

I've never faced the death of a spouse, but there were times I hurt so badly that I actually wished that B had just died. Somehow, if he weren't out there living a life without me, the loss of him would be easier to face. Watching Sonya's husband in the years following her death, I saw so many of my own emotions of sadness playing out again. What was different though, was the fact that Sonya's husband knew that wherever she was, she still loved him. I didn't have that. But I did have my life. Many times, when I didn't think I could get out of bed and face one more minute of heartbreak, when I wished the earth would swallow me up and let me escape the pain, I would think of Sonya and how badly she wanted to live. And

I'd remind myself that maybe I could find a reason, if just for that day. Then I'd put my feet on the floor, eyes puffy from a night of seemingly endless tears, and I'd face the day that I had been gifted.

Watching Sonya's battle for her physical life, even though a much bigger fight than the one I battle for my emotional life, is teaching me not only that there are reasons to live but also that I don't have to minimize or downplay my heartbreak to be a survivor. Sonya taught me that.

Chapter 25:
Eggs & Firemen

If you put a small value upon yourself, rest assured that the world will not raise your price.
—Anonymous

The only times I can remember being what I would call happy were when men who everyone else thought were cool, chose me. That means there were three times that I can remember feeling happy: Jason, Tyler, and B. It's a disturbing thought to feel like you aren't worth anything and can't be happy unless there's a man in your life. And not just any man. It has to be the popular one, the cute one that all the girls want. If I have that man, then I'm whole, then I'm complete, then I'm happy. But as my counselor pointed out, even when I had that man, I wasn't happy. Why? Because when real life settles in, and the excitement of the new relationship wears off, I'm still me. I'm still needy and wanting attention and love. I'm still desperate to find it in a form that makes sense to me, rather than look for and find it in what's right in front of me. I had the man I wanted ever since I was a child. He loved me. He chose me. But, as it turned out, that was only a temporary fill of the void.

When the demons returned, I blamed B. I wanted him to change. I needed him to change. Then he was gone, and I needed me to change. I had to prove to him that people can change. But then one night, talking with my little brother, he pointed out something I hadn't thought about. I was feeling the desperate need to change, but it wasn't really changing that I needed as much as it was discovering. I needed to figure out who in the heck I was. In the movie Runaway Bride, Julia Roberts' character had no idea how she liked her eggs because she would just order the same kind of eggs that the man in her life ordered. There's a scene with several different types of eggs on the table in front of her and she tastes them all and finally makes up her own mind. That always stuck with me. Even my mom sometimes would say, "You need to figure out what kind of eggs you like!" Thankfully, I know I like scrambled the best. But that may be one of the few things about myself that I'm sure of.

Lesson Learning: Find your values from within and own them too.

I've started trying to pay attention to things around me to determine if I like them. I'm learning that our bodies can tell us a lot if we learn to listen. In a counseling session, my counselor had me relax into a somewhat meditative state and then had me repeat statements she would make and see how they made me feel. These were related to my struggle with feeling restless in my job. She had me say things like, "It is important to me that I live geographically close to my family" or "It is important to me that I find enjoyment in coming to work." Sitting in her office, with nowhere to go and nothing else to do, I was able to focus on what was happening as I repeated her statements. Lo and behold, I could feel my body react, or not react at all. I could feel what was important, and I could recognize what I was indifferent about. It was fascinating! At one point, I even started to cry because I was so overcome by how strongly I felt about the statement I had just repeated! That experience was such a powerful lesson in the guidance we have in our own bodies to discover who we are. Everything I need in order to find myself is apparently in my own body. So, I try to remember to practice, even when I'm making little decisions, to listen to my body for guidance.

While that was a turning point, it continues to be a lesson I'm learning as I continue to find myself trying to be what I think others expect me to be. A recent experience, which was actually jam-packed with lessons learning, was being out with a girlfriend and having (literally for the first time in my life) a few guys approach us and ask to join us. Surprisingly, one of them had actually been looking at ME! Not my beautiful blonde friend, but ME! So what happens to poor attention-seeking Tiff? Well, she falls hook, line, and sinker, and she immediately shifts into "I need to be what this guy would think is cool" mode, whatever that is. In the conversation, I asked if he played sports, and he said he played football in high school. Then he asked me if I like to watch football. I froze. I couldn't care less about football. It's never been a sport I followed. I don't ever choose to watch it of my own volition (except the Super Bowl, which I watch mainly for the commercials, and so I can intelligently participate in the inevitable post-game water cooler conversations). So rather than being honest, I gave an ambiguous reply, "Yeah, I like to watch football sometimes." As long as one game a year counts as sometimes, then it wasn't entirely untrue. But it was me trying to be a pleaser. And then the lesson. "I hate watching football. I never watch it," he said. I almost laughed out loud at myself.

But the lesson wasn't over yet. I had the chance at that point to come clean and say that I really didn't like football either and was just trying to impress. But I kept up my lie for appearance's sake. After all, it was a fairly harmless lie and I didn't want to look wishy-washy. As it turned out, he and I were playing the same game. When he and his friends introduced themselves, they said they were firemen from Huntington Beach and were in Monterey for a conference. My friend looked them up the next day and found out they were policemen rather than firemen. Having exchanged numbers with the guy who picked me, when he later sent a text about work being busy, I asked if there were a lot of fires, and told him how my roommates and I had been rescued from an apartment fire while living in Huntington Beach and maybe he knew the guys. I was actually somewhat grateful that he wasn't really a fireman and couldn't know the guys that rescued us because that would have meant he could have been privy to the aforementioned toothpaste story. But his dishonesty was still annoying.

To my surprise and total disappointment, he kept up the charade and made some comment about there not being a lot of fires but how firemen these days were mostly medical personnel anyway. I was mad! I called him out. I beat him up about it. Even when he told me he was sorry and that they had just decided to use that story because people seem to like firemen and dislike cops, I couldn't let it go. I told him how disappointed I was that he had been dishonest and how it invalidated anything else he had said. And then, shocker, I stopped hearing from him. Only later did I put together the fact that, while maybe on a smaller scale, I had done the exact same thing he had done by pretending to be somebody I wasn't. Pot meets kettle.

I guess the point of all of this is that while I may continue to stumble in my progress, each time I recognize it, I'm armed with more knowledge for the next time, and the next time, and the next time. The possibility still exists that I'll fall into the same trap, but it also exists that the next time, I'll own the fact that I don't like football, or sushi, or fish of pretty much any kind, or golf, or hunting, or whatever. Finding value from within is a two-pronged attack. First, figure out what you like, who you are, what you believe. Second, own it. I'm still discovering, but learning to own my findings.

Chapter 26:
Please Validate Me!

Remembering that some women marry death-row pen pals reminds me that my life choices aren't so bad after all.—**Unknown**

I always prided myself on being a happy single person, which is a little silly since I wasn't really happy single or married. It was more about my satisfaction in the fact that I wasn't ever one of those girls who was pining away to get married. I figured marriage would come when it came. But after going to grad school and then spending several years out in the work force, I found myself in an interesting place. I didn't really want to get married, but I didn't necessarily want to be alone. Cohabitation wasn't an option, but I hadn't met anyone who was interested enough to get to a point where that conversation would even be warranted. I didn't want to be married, but I was starting to feel like no one would ever want me, and that seemed unpalatable as well. It was a quandary for sure.

The situation was amplified by the fact that I believed my worth was determined by whether or not I had a man in my life, so having gone such a long time without anyone giving me even a second glance, I was feeling pretty worthless at that point. I found myself instead creating a duplicitous life to add some excitement and to feel desirable. I found men who were not relationship material but would give me the time of day, and I kept my involvement with them a secret from everyone else in my life. Because I didn't see them as potential partners, I didn't feel like I was jeopardizing anything. And this way, at least I had someone in my life who found me attractive, and the secrecy kept it exciting.

One way I knew that I still had a long way to go after my divorce was that I fell into this same pattern soon after. But this time, I felt even more desperation to be desired. After all, I was at the lowest point I'd ever been on the scale of self-worth. I believed that if B were with someone and I wasn't, then not only was he right about me, but it would then become obvious to everyone who knew us that I was the problem. After all, he had gone right into a successful relationship. I couldn't get a date. Therefore, I was the one who wasn't relationship material. I was the undesirable one. So I became a little obsessive in my desire to prove that I could get a man.

This was a ridiculously unhealthy way to deal with divorce or any breakup. When B told me he was done, it was like a light went on in my head and I could see myself as he had over the last few years. All my glaring weaknesses, all my judgments of him, my unpredictable moods, my constant state of discontent, my misplaced belief that his actions could make me happy. I could see it all in full view. I tried over and over to explain to him that I could see now what had happened, that I understood why he became unhappy, that I knew I could be different and how completely and utterly sorry I was. I begged and pleaded and reasoned and cried. I didn't realize at the time that he had left me in his mind long before he told me, so by the time he said the words to me, he was already long gone. What I also didn't realize at that point was that I had a lot more to learn before I was really ready to be a partner to him or anyone else. I'd like to think that I could have learned the lessons and kept my marriage together but honestly, I don't know if that would have been possible. Maybe the only way for me to internalize the lessons was to hit the most incredible low I could imagine. Maybe if staying as I was became distasteful enough, I would be ready to do the hard work to change.

Lesson Learning: You can still move forward and "live" without another man/relationship (but don't run off and join a convent!)

As much as I wanted to meet someone, to prove my worth, the idea of dating again made me sick. I can't say much has changed about that over the years. Even today, the idea of dating makes me a little nauseous. Especially because I'm super insistent about not wasting time. And let's face it, dating can be a lot of wasted time. Having to face dating again angered me even more because B didn't have to do it. I don't know where I got the idea that things should be fair, but nothing about that was fair. No awkward first dates. No facing the online dating monster question: will I or won't I? And if I will, will I tell anyone? I, along with many others I'm sure, could write a bestselling book about the horrors of online dating. But hey, online is where I made my friend who brought me his last marijuana bud during cancer. I'll always have the Internet to thank for that.

Learning that I could move forward, that I could be alone for the rest of my life and not be seen as inferior for having a failed marriage and then no successful relationship after, has not been easy. Maybe getting to the "screw what everyone else thinks; I'm awesome" phase is not even possible with my psychological makeup. But what I'm learning is this: if I believe that I'm inferior or that other people think I'm inferior, then I'll always feel inferior. If you're not an inherently confident person, then to gain confidence, you have to feign confidence. Sort of. The reality is that, for all the things I tell myself about what a loser I am if I don't find a man who's way cooler, way hotter, and way more successful than B, there are facts that can refute those things. I won't kid you, these facts sometimes take me a while to dig up. But they exist. Do I know people who got divorced and haven't remarried but are pretty awesome? Yes.

Fact: Not all people who get divorced and don't remarry are losers. I used to say that I was plain and had never been picked out of a crowd, but even that finally happened once. Granted I was in my 40s when it finally did, but fact: I've now been picked out of a crowd, which means I'm not entirely unattractive or unnoticeable.

Fact: There are many advantages to being single. My married friends say how they envy me sometimes when they have a husband to answer to, kids who have 24-7 needs, and no time for themselves. I've got quite a bit of time for myself. Maybe I haven't figured out all the best ways to use it, but it's mine and no one else's. I have no idea what it's like to live in a house full of kids, or to have to wonder who used something last and where they might have put it. (Okay, I don't have to wonder who the last one was to use it, but I still have to wonder sometimes where I put it.) The point is, the grass always seems greener on the other side of the marriage fence. And I'm notorious for wanting what I can't have. Thankfully, I have time to practice wanting what I do have. Life ain't over till it's over. And mine ain't over.

It feels so much better to think about all the things I can add to my life that are only possible because I'm single, or at least a whole lot easier to accomplish being single! It makes me focus a lot less on my biological clock and geriatric ovaries and a lot more on how much I can do as a single person before I potentially meet someone. The list is getting longer and longer, so it might just take me until the end of my life to complete. Perfect! Then single or not, my situation is a win-win.

Lesson Learning: The grass is always greener where you water it.

As easy as that may sound, it all comes back to being okay with the way things are right now. No doubt loneliness can be incredibly painful, but finding ways to be with it and even find humor in it can be good medicine. For example, soon after B and I moved into the house we couldn't afford, I ordered address labels. I usually just use the free ones that come from the local animal shelter, so this was a splurge. They had a stick figure man, woman, and dog and said "The Allen Family." We weren't great letter writers so there were still sheets of them after B left. I'm not sure if it was Sentimental Tiff or Tight Wad Tiff who couldn't get rid of them but rather than throw them out, I decided they could still be used. Before sending them out however, I would put a circle with a line through it around the man and another around the dog and write R.I.P near the dog. Then I would cross out "Family" so it just said "The Allen." I got a kick out of sending them to friends and family that I knew would get a laugh. Making something humorous out of them makes me smile and in those moments, it becomes a little easier to make peace with what is.

Chapter 27:
Happiness Project &
Hypnotist

But if these years have taught me anything it is this: you can never run away. Not ever. The only way out is in.—**Junot Diaz**

When Gretchen Rubin started The Happiness Project, she wanted to see if she could change her level of happiness in her normal, everyday life. She wasn't able to travel the world or escape in any way. The idea was that she could make an extraordinary difference in her life by making small changes. That's exactly how I felt when I started writing. I wanted to show that finding yourself doesn't need to involve something huge and transformative. I worried that without some major event or even being able to say I had reached a destination and found myself, no one would be interested in my story. But maybe you're wondering if you can get through whatever it is you're facing without the ability or even the need to run away from it. Hang in there! I'm living proof that it's possible!

Lesson Learning: You can find yourself without running away.

You can find yourself in little choices you make every day. You can find yourself by taking small moments to reflect and tune in to what your body is telling you. Because when you can become aware of what your body is telling you, then you've tapped into your intuition. You've tapped into your true self.

When I worked as a nursing home administrator, we had a hypnotist come to a company meeting one year. I was one of the participants. I loved hypnotist shows and had tried to be chosen anytime I went to one, but I was always so high-strung that I could never be hypnotized. This time was different. B and I were dating, I was doing a job I really enjoyed, and overall I was in a pretty good place. I was able to relax enough to actually get hypnotized. I had always wondered how it worked, how it felt. I guess it's different for everyone, but I was totally aware of what was happening and what I was doing. The difference was that I just didn't care. I didn't care who was watching or what people thought. I felt free. When I was told that I was a vacuum cleaner, I got down on the floor to be the best little vacuum I could be. When I was told that the person next to me was cold and I needed to warm them, I had no problem climbing right on top of them. They would not be cold on my watch! When I was told that upon hearing a certain word, I was to give that person a hug, I ran and jumped into the arms of a coworker with everything I had, to give the biggest hug ever known. (I suppose this may also show my alarming need to be the best at everything!) I was so hypnotized that when the show ended, people noticed that I was still acting strangely. I was still clinging to anyone who said the word. I was staring off and not able to focus. The company's legal counsel eventually called the hypnotist to ask him what to do. The answer was to get me outside in fresh air and give it time, which did the trick.

Looking back, I've thought about how amazing I felt that night. I came to the conclusion that it was the result of finally being able to be myself without any concern about how others perceived me. I felt completely liberated and free. I was still me, still wanting to be the best at everything, but I wasn't desperate for anyone to notice. I was just doing it for me. I wasn't looking around at everyone else to see if I was the best vacuum. I was just focused on being the best vacuum I could be. And being the best vacuum I could be was good enough for me. Pretty insightful stuff from an altered state of consciousness.

I thought that in order to heal, I needed to find myself so I could be myself. And I thought the only way I would ever accomplish that was to embark on some crazy, off-the-wall, life-altering adventure in some far-off country. But I'm learning that it doesn't take a year in the Peace Corps, a trip around the world, running away to join the circus, or finding a whole new career. In fact, one of the biggest lessons I'm learning is that those who find peace, happiness, and gratitude in their current circumstances are more likely to dream big and turn those dreams into reality. I'm not saying it makes complete sense to me yet, but it certainly seems to have substantiated truth. So maybe I don't need to run away; maybe this is more of what my brother alluded to, an inner journey of self-discovery. But sometimes that huge hole that B left seems too big to ignore. What about that?

Chapter 28:
Mama Bunny & Map Theory

You yourself, as much as anyone else in the Universe, deserve your love and affection.
—**Buddha**

One of the most difficult lessons, and I'm learning that it's among the most valuable, is accepting that I'm right where I'm meant to be. Call it a divine plan, a life mission, or an individual blueprint, we're all here for a purpose. And wherever we are on our path, we are there because we are meant to be there for our growth and development. This means grasping the concept that there really are no accidents. We are too complex, too well-developed, and too powerful to not be creatures of a higher purpose. And if that's the case, then I am right where I'm meant to be.

But here's another difficult thing to accept. If it's true that I'm right where I'm meant to be, then it would follow that B is right where he's meant to be as well. With all my wanting him to be wrong, wanting him to discover somehow that his choice was a mistake, I cannot have it both ways. If I am where I'm meant to be, then so is he. That's a difficult pill to swallow. But it's a far healthier pill than agonizing about how this was all wrong and everything in life is now messed up because of it. Certainly it's not a road I would have chosen. But what if I could have compassion for myself? What if I could be kind to the girl who hasn't healed but is healing, who isn't changed but is changing, who hasn't arrived but is arriving? What if I could love the girl who is at least progressing and growing, and even love the girl who stagnates for a while and periodically feels like giving up?

Lesson Learning: You're right where you're meant to be. Be your own mama bunny.

My counselor had me read a book once that I actually remembered from my childhood. I now keep a copy on my nightstand. It's called The Runaway Bunny by Margaret Wise Brown. It's the story of a little bunny who tells his mother that he's running away. No matter where he tells her he will run, she tells him she will follow. If he becomes a fish in a stream to swim away, she will become a fisherman and fish for him. If he becomes a rock on a high mountain, she will become a mountain climber and climb to him. If he becomes a bird and flies away, she will become a tree that he can come home to. On and on it goes until the little bunny finally decides that it would just be easier to stay home and be her little bunny.

When I read it out loud in that counseling session, I was totally overcome with emotion. All I could think about was my own mom and the millions of ways she has rescued me over the years. She has literally saved my life. But then another thought crept in. What if I could be my own mama bunny? What if I could love my inner child the way the mama bunny loved the baby bunny? Then, if I remain alone the rest of my life, when my mom and dad are gone, no matter what circumstances may come, I could come to my own rescue. I could love the baby bunny in me, even as it thought about running away to find itself. I could be my own mama bunny.

This thought was incredibly hopeful to me. If I could learn how to catch myself when I fall, love myself when I fail and accept myself in my own stubbornness, then all the seeking for external validation, all the need to be the favorite, all the debilitating feelings of inadequacy would just fade away. I certainly wasn't expecting I could get to the point where I'd never have those needs or feelings again, but just the slight hope that I could get even a moment of relief from them opened the floodgates for me. But, how to get there? Even if possible, it seems like a mountain with a treacherous climb.

It seems almost ironic that accepting how things are is a necessary first step toward discovering or changing anything. Accepting what is means that I need to stop fighting against my reality because I don't like it or because I want it to be different. When my counselor first told me that, I wanted my copay back. It made zero sense to me. If I accepted how things are, then I wouldn't be motivated to change them. Duh! But as it turns out, we can spend a whole lot of energy beating ourselves up for things we don't like, things that we "should" do differently or feel differently about, or see differently. We can waste a lot of energy on being angry about circumstances not being what we want them to be. Sometimes, we think we deserve better. Sometimes, we think we deserve worse. Either way, it's a whole lot of brain cells that are kept so busy stressing about how things "should" be that there is no space for ideas to come in, little nuggets that might be found in a quiet moment and crack open a door to discovery that we thought was bolted shut. I can't say I've had any of this grand revelation necessarily, but in the briefest of moments, when I'm able to let myself accept things as they are, and me as I am, it's a whole lot more peaceful in my head and in my body.

Lesson Learning: You can't know which direction to go until you know where you're starting from.

My counselor described it like this. She asked me to pick a place in the U.S. that I wanted to see. I picked North Carolina. Then the kicker. If I wanted to go to North Carolina, how would I know which direction to go if I didn't know from where I was starting? I can't know which direction to take to my destination unless I know where I'm at right now. Finally, a light bulb went on that helped me see the idea behind accepting where I'm at, discovering who I am right now, and then being able to potentially reach a new destination.

Chapter 29:
Hard & Sailor

Do not pray for easy lives. Pray to be stronger men. Do not pray for tasks equal to your powers. Pray for powers equal to your tasks. Then the doing of your work shall be no miracle, but you shall be the miracle.
—Phillips Brooks (1835–1893)

When I faced the reality of my divorce, I felt like life as I knew it was over. I would never be the same again. The truth is, I was right. Something inside inherently changed when I had to keep getting up every day. Something changed when I had to figure out how to deal with three upside down mortgages as well as how to take care of rentals, fix things, evict tenants, and find new tenants. Something changed when I faced cancer with no one to curl up to and hold me at night. Something changed when I had to figure out on my own what to do when my car broke down, when the roof leaked, when I couldn't seem to stop crying. I would never be the same again. Instead, I was becoming stronger. I had been independent for years before I was married, but this time I had to do it on a much grander scale and I had to do it through the most painful and crushing period of my life. I was sure it would never end. I was sure that I would never live another day without wallowing in sadness, regret, anger, fatigue, and failure. All I knew to do was put one foot in front of the other. Make decisions as they were needed. I spent a lot of time mourning the past and agonizing about the future. I spent a lot of time reading everything I could find on how to change me, how to make me whole, how to make me an optimist.

If I were dropped back into the middle of it again, I'd probably still struggle to see any light. It's just always so dark when you're in the depths of it. And it can last awhile. When B told me that leaving and divorcing me was hard for him, I nearly flipped out. In my mind, he had no idea what hard was. Did he go to bed and wake up alone? Did he have dreams of intimacy and love and then wake up to cold emptiness? Did he lose 25 pounds in two months and have globs of hair fall out? Did he face all this living in a place with no close friends and family and while trying to work two jobs? He had the luxury of crawling into another woman's bed, of going to Tucson where he was surrounded by friends and close to family. Sure, I'd like to think it was a hard decision for him to leave, a hard decision to divorce. I would hope so. But it would have been harder for him to stay and face what had happened to us. Leaving was the easier choice.

His mom would later say that when she asked him why he chose M instead of me, he told her simply that being with M was easy. After hearing that, I did a lot of thinking about easy vs. hard. When given the option, who wouldn't choose easy, right? Easy is . . . well, EASIER! I kept a post-it note in my bathroom for months that was put up by some good friends. It said, "Hard is not bad. Hard is just hard." I think it's pretty obvious to most of us that life really isn't necessarily easy or fair, but oftentimes there are easier paths to choose. So why in the world do we plug along through hard? What draws us away from just coasting down the path of least resistance?

Lesson Learning: Hard things in life mold us, refine us, build us, strengthen us, and prepare us.

I've always been afraid of hard. Hard is scary. Hard is unknown. Hard can be overwhelming. Hard can be too much. Hard is for strong people. The idea of hard sometimes makes me hyperventilate. Then hard stuff happened. I remember saying during my divorce that I was already scared to death of the next time I was ever going to have to feel like that. It was just too much. Yet, somehow, I came out on the other side. Not only that, but my eyes were being opened in ways they never had been before. I was different. I was stronger. Then cancer. As I've mentioned, although for me it wasn't nearly as hard as divorce, it certainly caused some angst and tears. To this day I tell people that cancer was easy; it was divorce that almost killed me. I can't help but wonder if cancer didn't feel as hard because of the strength I gained from the divorce. Maybe it was the first hard thing that made the next hard thing easier! Maybe it's the hard things that mold us, refine us, build us, strengthen us, and prepare us!

So this is what I'm learning . . . I WANT easy, but I NEED hard. Hard builds character. Hard stretches me and makes me swim in deeper waters. But I'm still in the process of learning that hard doesn't have to mean unhappy. Perspective is everything. Commitment is everything. Patience is everything. So how do I get to the point of being unshakeable in the midst of hard? The Catch-22 is that it takes hard things to begin to make me unshakeable. Surviving through hard is satisfying and rewarding. Am I ready to ask for strength like the quote at the beginning of this chapter? Well, probably not yet. Do I still need to learn more coping skills to get through the hard things that are most certainly in my future? Oh yeah. Do I still need to continue to learn how to be the very best I can be in the midst of hard without letting self-absorption creep in? Most definitely. And do I need to learn not to create hard unnecessarily? You bet! But when hard comes now, I'm feeling much more ready to try and embrace it, to do my best to not be too afraid of it or run from it. I'm learning to think about the person I can become and the more solid relationships I can have on the other side of hard.

In January 2015, a plane crashed in the woods of Kentucky and seven-year-old Sailor Gutzler was the only survivor. Killed in the crash were her parents and sister as well as a cousin. With no shoes on her feet, dressed only in shorts and a T-shirt on a cold winter night, and with a broken wrist, she headed into the wooded darkness. She finally saw a light and worked her way toward it. But between her and the light was three-quarters of a mile of thorns, briars, creek beds, and embankments. She fought her way through all of it however, and found a friendly face at the light, a man who took her in, cleaned her up and got help for her. She fought through treacherous terrain, fear and darkness to get to the small light that most likely was not even constantly visible to her. Her body was beat up in the process. She was facing a horrible loss. But she found her way to safety and in so doing, saved her own life. I'm sure Sailor will never be the same again. And although my circumstances were much less traumatic than Sailor's, I too am trying to fight my way through difficult and unknown terrain toward a light that dips and wanes, but that I finally believe is there because I've caught glimpses of it.

It's true, I'll never be the same again. And I never want to be. Hard is making me better.

Chapter 30: Three-Pronged Forgiveness

Forgiveness . . . means taking what happened seriously and not minimizing it; drawing out the sting in the memory that threatens to poison our entire existence. It involves trying to understand the perpetrators and so have empathy, to try to stand in their shoes and appreciate the sort of pressures and influences that might have conditioned them.—**Desmond Tutu**

Although probably already painfully obvious, one of the most difficult processes of healing is forgiveness. Honestly, this sometimes feels next to impossible. However, I heard once that not forgiving was like drinking poison and expecting the other person to die. That just sounds plain dumb. But I confess I've been drinking poison for way too long. Even wanting to forgive is a start, but I told myself I wanted to forgive long before I really truly wanted to. I thought if I forgave B, then somehow that let him off the hook. Somehow, if I didn't hurt as much or suffer as much, then he wouldn't have as much bad karma coming his way. And my vengeful, childish self wanted bad karma for him. At one point, I was given the suggestion to pray for him for two weeks. I'm pretty sure the first week was entirely through gritted teeth, but after a while, I could actually say the words without as much sarcasm. Even more interesting was that, as I did this, I found myself more easily able to forgive others. Slowly, I'm learning that forgiveness is possible. This gives me hope that I can and will be able to forgive the biggest hurt of all. It's coming. I'm starting to believe it.

But forgiveness isn't just about the parties who wronged you. I needed to forgive myself. As it turns out, this is just as hard as trying to forgive B, if not harder. Even at 32-years-old, I went into marriage with completely unrealistic expectations. I didn't realize I had them right away, but I had them. I grew up believing that, since my parents had one of the most solid relationships I was privy to, then in order for my own marriage to be successful, it needed to look like theirs. It was naïve, and truthfully pretty selfish.

When the sentimental, giddy, excited part of B seemed to fizzle soon after we got married, I focused my attention on how he had changed and paid very little attention to the fact that I was changing too. I had always believed that you could just "be yourself" in your marriage and your partner was supposed to love you no matter what. I thought I was trying to be a good wife, but I also wanted him to love and cherish me even when I wasn't.

My mom told me once that even as a stay-at-home mom, she tried to look presentable when my dad got home. It wasn't because she thought he expected it, and he certainly didn't, but it was her way of showing that she both loved and respected him and wanted him to know that he was worth making the effort. I thought that was so beautiful. Unfortunately, I heard this (and many other important keys to a successful marriage) far too late, though I'm not sure that any good advice I received during my marriage would have even sunk in. I was so wrapped up in what I needed that I didn't consider him. I failed him, just as I thought he was failing me. Though I thought I was behaving otherwise, his needs were always second to my own.

Before we were married, I loved to surprise him. I drove the six hours from Huntington Beach once and left red Swedish fish stuck to the door of his work. Then I hid and watched as the realization came over him of what they meant, and he looked around crazily trying to figure out where I was. I had so much fun bringing that kind of joy to him while we were dating. I honestly don't remember any surprises I did for him after we were married. Not one.

I've literally spent years thinking about what happened to us, what happened to the "all-American" couple who promised forever to each other. Where did the optimistic guy go who was sure we could make a wonderful life together? Where did the girl go who finally let herself feel safe, could finally put one foot in front of the other toward the altar and was getting the fairy tale ending of doing it with her childhood crush?

The problem with these questions is that trying to find answers to them keeps me stuck in the past. Ideally, I want to glean the lessons from my failed marriage and then charge ahead with a renewed effort to not make the same mistakes again. It sounds fairly straightforward, but my regrets are deep.

Lesson Learning: Forgiveness is three-pronged. 1) Whether you receive it or

not, you need to ask for it. 2) Whether they ask for it or not, you need to give it. 3) No matter what mistakes you made, gift yourself with it because you deserve it.

One comfort I have is that, in the dark hours after B's announcement, I asked for his forgiveness. I pled for it. Maybe it was way too late, and that's a lesson I hope to never forget, but with all the sincerity of my heart, I told him all the ways I was wrong and asked him to please forgive me. He couldn't at the time, and I remember asking him to let me know when he was able to. Although I don't know if that ever happened, I know that I did the best I could, admitting fault and apologizing for the role I had played in our downfall. Whether he ever forgave me, or will ever forgive me, is no longer a weight around me. I asked sincerely, apologetically, and honestly.

As for the other two prongs, I'll keep working to forgive myself for the many ways I drove B away just as I work to forgive him for giving up on me. The difference now is that I know this can happen. I've already been able to see a clearer picture of what he must have seen when he decided to leave. I can now see that he must have felt he had tried everything in his power, that he had done the best he possibly could. That thought helps me to see myself as having also tried the best I could with the knowledge I had at the time. Seeing two people who tried their best, taking into account their upbringing, their unique personalities, and their life experiences makes it a little easier to forgive them both. And forgiving them both is absolutely crucial.

Chapter 31: Let It Be

Suffering is overrated.—Bill Veeck

One of the phrases that I've grown to hate (although it still comes out of my mouth way more than I'd like to admit) is "Let it go." This will seem ironic to some who know that I get the Frozen song stuck in my head and have been known to sing it at the top of my lungs. I do love that song. But what I prefer is John Lennon's take, "Let it be."

I read the most beautiful blog (www.mindfulhub.com), written by Donna Torney posted in "40 Days of Letting Go" on Oct 3, 2015. There was no way to paraphrase her words and do them any justice. So with her kind permission, here they are:

> Some life events cause a distinct chasm—on one side stands "before," on the other side "after." The deeper the chasm, the more desperately we may try to get back to "before." Chronic illness, a break-up, addiction, the death of a loved one. When we can't accept a situation, we might try frantically to change it, reeling against it,

trying to control the outcome. We might be so intent on fighting the reality of the situation that we inadvertently cause more pain.

Has anyone ever told you to "let it go" when you were in deep pain? Did this feel like a slap in the face, cause a surge of anger, leave you feeling misunderstood, even more alone? . . . if this has happened to you, you're actually not alone.

If you have experienced this reaction in the face of the well-meaning "let it go" advice-giver, chances are you are experiencing a grief so deep that letting go is not an option. This is where letting it be comes into play.

Last spring I attended a weekend retreat on grief with a friend who experienced the sudden loss of her son. We talked about the awful slap in the face of being told to "let it go." My friend said, "Letting it go implies it's gone . . . but it's not gone. Letting it be is coming to terms with what is and not beating yourself up over what was or what could have been."

In contrast to letting it go, Letting it be builds a bridge over the chasm of before and after, as opposed to futile attempts to fill in the chasm. Letting it be allows moments of peace during a situation that we can't, but may desperately want to escape. It allows a brief respite to consider the possibility of feeling reconnected . . . to a loved one, a community, to the here-and-now . . . to something bigger. Letting it be comes and goes, but it presents a moment of mindfulness . . . and the possibility of a good life in spite of the chasm.

For most of us the ability to Let it Be comes and goes. With small doses of letting it be we can start to build an altered, but good life, perhaps even enjoying the journey. Like power and powerlessness, letting it be makes room for real peace, one moment, sometimes one second at a time.

Thank you, Donna. I couldn't have said it better.

Chapter 32:
Changing Perceptions

I'm single. You'll have to be freaking amazing to change that.—**Unknown**

I love Disney movies. I love Hallmark channel movies. Unless I'm having a love sucks day, I love to have my heartstrings tugged by a good fairy tale ending. When I started writing, I had no idea how this book would end. I had no fairy tale ending. In fact, my fairy tale had suffered a terrible death. I knew I would never have another fairy tale since I'm pretty sure they're rationed to only one per person per lifetime. It seems some people get overlooked entirely, so I suppose I was among the lucky ones to even be on the list. But if I reached my quota of fairy tale endings by age 35, then how in the world can I ever live happily ever after? Maybe your answer to this question is similar to what mine was. There is no such thing as happily ever after. Happy endings are fake. While I'll admit, I'm still somewhat skeptical now and then, there is a myriad of research to show that our thoughts create our reality. If that's the case, then I don't need a fairy tale ending to live happily ever after. I just need to do some pretty extensive mental work. Don't get me wrong. I wish there was a pill or a potion. But at least there's an option.

Lesson Learning: You don't need a fairy tale ending to live happily ever after.

If you haven't realized it by now, I'm a bit of a hot mess. I'm not happy about it. But at least I'm not as angry about it these days. It's all part of self-discovery. I can't lose hot mess status until I own that it exists. So we're becoming better acquainted. I'm learning what exactly creates the hot mess in my head and in my life and all roads lead back to my thoughts, my perceptions, and what I choose to believe about any given event or situation. Why is it that B's mom wrote "Mr. Happy" on the back of his sixth-grade picture that she gave to me one day at the ripe old age of nine? Because this gift of putting a positive twist on everything came naturally to him. But I was a different story. I was going to have to work for it. I will most likely be working on it until my last breath. But the alternative to doing the work is no longer an option for me.

The path of wallowing in misery, as I learned during my stint in the land of the mental meltdown folks, is actually the easier path for those of us who were born assuming the glass is and always will be half empty. Facing the hard work of retraining my mind and breaking forty or so years of bad habits seemed way too overwhelming to me. And how in the world do you change your perception of things that are just inherently bad? Luckily, other than divorce, cancer, and the dark days at that first nursing home, I have led a relatively unscathed life. But if I look back, I can see many seemingly small events that, had I been able to choose a healthier perception, may have prepped me for the bigger whammies that were coming my way.

I can't do much about any of that now but I can, however, start practicing for my future. I started my practice with a pet peeve of mine, bad drivers. When some little hot car whips in front of me without signaling to catch the freeway exit we've nearly passed, I say in my head, "Poor guy must be late for work and totally stressed out." I make up all kinds of stories and excuses until I'm practically laughing out loud at how elaborate they are. It's just a little trick. Then, when the only cute guy at a singles event that my girlfriend dragged me to ended up choosing her after I tried in vain to have a conversation with him, I found myself thinking, "Well, she has four kids. She needs to find someone more than I do." Maybe this Jedi mind stuff really does work! And the most exciting part is that since I decide how I perceive events, then I choose my happy ending and I can stop waiting for the next fairy tale or Prince Charming. I can just do my best to keep putting in the time and effort to find the happy in whatever comes my way. It's not easy. I'm learning it takes a ton of discipline, hard work, practice, and compassion for failure, but if I can choose to not obsess when I'm not picked by the cute guy and not go straight into how ugly and awful I am, there definitely has been progress.

As I began to reframe my thoughts in order to perceive things in a more positive light, I could feel a subtle shift. I'm not bouncing off the walls with joy by any means, but I've always been the victim of "when this happens, I'll be happy," or "when that changes, I'll be happy." By changing my perception, I'm free to find happy now and I don't need to have it be linked to some future event.

After the divorce, I learned that B felt like every time he would hit some bar I had set, I would raise the bar. He could never win. Tragically, that's how I've lived a lot of my life. When I cleared certain goal posts, I realized I still wasn't happy, so I was already looking ahead to the next one. It's a vicious cycle, and I sucked B right into it. The sad part is, I got my fairy tale ending but I still wasn't happy! Tragic. An epic fail on my part. But after years of feeling the desperate need to be given a chance to go back and change it, I'm finally starting to see it with new eyes. These eyes see the truth that I was doing the best I could based on who I was in that moment. These eyes allow me to cut that girl a little slack for her choices while gently reminding her that there are no do-overs. These eyes allow her to see that she doesn't have to have a fairy tale ending to live happily ever after.

Conclusion

While I may not be completely recovered from my experiences, I'm certainly recovering. I am learning. I am growing. I am changing. No matter what B believed about me, no matter what he had to tell himself about me being unable to change to justify his actions, he was wrong about one big thing. I can change. But to know which direction to go, I must first figure out where I'm starting from. I must figure out who I am. And once I have a grasp on that, then I'm free to choose my destination and start down the path of change.

B will go on and live his life. He and M may be together for the rest of their lives. They may not. In the end, my goal is to stop having my nose stuck up against that closed door. Ever so slowly, I am turning around. Even if my ex-husband still enters my mind every day, he no longer enters it every hour, every minute, every second, as he did in the initial darkness and in so many months that followed. As with every other part of this journey, the change has been gradual, nearly imperceptible. But today, I look back and I see the progress.

I thought the only way to survive it was to fill the void with someone else. As it turns out, survival doesn't require that the void be filled. Sure, I sometimes still feel like the fact that I'm single means I'm not relationship material, that I'm damaged goods. Well, I am damaged goods. But I'm still goods. When I feel myself going down that rabbit hole in my brain, I have two choices. I can let my brain run with it. (I can't lie; sometimes, that's exactly what happens.) But more and more often, I'm choosing the second option. The one where I yell, "STOP!" in my head (or sometimes even out loud), and I redirect my thoughts. I redirect them to some place better, some place healthier. I mourn the facts, but I let the stories go, and I'll be mama bunny to that girl who keeps trying.

I am learning to want B's happiness. I am learning to forgive him. I am learning to forgive myself. I am learning to let it be. I am learning to move on. But there are times when he can still conjure up such overwhelming emotion in me. Good or bad, it's my reality. As I continue on my journey of life and of healing, I will carry on, but I'm learning to leave my excess baggage behind. I will bring with me only that baggage that is a natural result of my experiences, the lessons I'm learning. But the baggage I create for myself, I will most definitely leave behind. I'm learning that it's not worth paying the extra price it costs to drag it with me. I look ahead to feeling lighter and lighter until the day when I realize I'm traveling with just me, and I am enough.

TO BE CONTINUED

Life may seem half over

at age 41,

But come follow my journey,

I'm not nearly done.

www.tiffany-allen.com

Editor Outtakes

As a first time author, I had no idea what to expect from the writing, editing and publishing process. I assumed that editing in particular would be somewhat humbling, but I was in for a surprise. I chose Wayne Purdin, a highly recommended editor, and also had my own mother do a run through.

Lesson Learning: Becoming a published author requires a thick skin.

In the end, I was incredibly grateful for all the feedback (and reading recommendations), but with permission from both my editor and my mom, I wanted to share some of the comments that came back on my various drafts. Please enjoy my "Editor Outtakes."

Editor: A separation ritual by itself doesn't have any power. It has to accompany some self-revelation . . . Maybe you need to realize that even though you may be legally divorced from B, you aren't psychologically divorced.

Re: "I'm writing this for me"

Editor: Not entirely, otherwise it would just be a journal.

Editor: I don't think you're being totally honest. You're not telling readers the whole truth about your role in driving B away from you. You present it like it was all his fault and that you can't understand how someone who once adored you suddenly left and went to live with another woman. If you change this to an understanding of how B felt with you constantly harping about money, then you won't have to worry about people being hurt or angry.

Editor: Chapter 25 had too much crazy. Other chapters had enough crazy. And it didn't have a lesson for readers. This chapter needs more about how you need to forgive yourself and ask B for forgiveness. Base it on Tutu's quote.

Editor: I don't see how saying that you're still holding onto the CD, video, and ring will help readers let go of the past and move on with their lives. It's true that some sentimental people like you require more time. But you should say here that eventually you have to let go of these things. Read Melanie Beatty's Co-Dependent No More.

Editor: Chapter 27's story is cute, but where's the lesson? It's just more sentimental stuff that you should have thrown away years ago. Chapter 28 belongs in a journal or at the bottom of the Mediterranean. It doesn't help the reader because it's addressed to B. Readers already understand your obsession with B and don't need another seven pages of it.

Editor: Did you say you were sorry and ask for forgiveness? Realizing you made mistakes isn't enough to heal from a breakup and move on. Read Zero Limits by Dr. Joe Vitale.

Mom: This chapter contains WAY too much of the same crap. You've said all this before. It feels like beating a dead horse, too much overkill. Get rid of all this maudlin drama. Because I know you, I find your honesty about wanting to be rich and famous etc. somewhat endearing but when I read it here as a reader, I find it very off-putting.

Mom: Once again you have launched into redundant, unhelpful, uninteresting territory. I can tell this chapter came at the end of your writing experience when you yourself said that it just got to be an exercise in spewing. I have taken much out.

The editing process certainly stung a bit. But thank you Wayne. Thank you Mom. Because of both of you, this book may stand a fighting chance.

Acknowledgements

As a child, my parents taught us to write thank you notes for birthday gifts, Christmas gifts, and pretty much everything in between. I used to think it was such a tedious process, but as I ponder the many people who contributed in some way to this book coming to fruition, I am overwhelmed with gratitude. I only wish this "thank you note" could in some small way accurately convey what is in my heart.

Thank you to Caring Bridge for giving me an outlet to begin writing, and to all the readers of my Caring Bridge blog who kept telling me I was funny and should write a book. I would never have put fingers to keyboard without you.

Thank you to Chandler Bolt for producing enthusiastic and motivating videos for Self-Publishing School that made me believe I could actually become an author and then got this tight-wad to drop some money for the course, which kicked the "I have to get my money's worth" juices into flow and created accountability.

Thank you to Megan Jamison, my Self-Publishing School coach, who could talk me down from the ledges every time I wanted to quit and continued to show support above and beyond her "required" duties.

Thank you to my wonderful "Accountabilibuddy" from Self-Publishing School, Judith Pratt-Jeffries. From thousands of miles away, you held my feet to the fire each week and reminded me that together, we could do this.

Thank you to my book launch team for keeping me motivated and excited and helping boost my confidence just by wanting to be a part of this journey.

Thank you to my editors, Wayne Purdin and my Mom, for turning my long-winded rants into a more condensed and rational narration and for agreeing to allow me to include their Editor Outtakes.

Thank you to Happy Publishing for my book cover and Angie Mroczka for the formatting.

Thank you to Donna Torney, who graciously allowed me to use her blog post from www.mindfulhub.com.

Thank you to all the family, friends, and co-workers who had to watch and listen to me work through all of these experiences, each of them hopeful but not entirely sure it would ever end.

Thank you to my nieces (Kali, Mali, Shayla, and Macy) and my nephews (Cameron, Cayman, Koslan, Korovin, Kodiak, & Kenai) for giving me good stories to tell and for always loving Aunt T. I'm so proud to be your aunt and I love you more than you will ever know.

Thank you to Tiffany Yant (T1) and Sonya McLaren for inspiring me to live after cancer, and Sonya's nephew, Austin Fitch who gave me purpose during Sonya's passing and who, in continuing to remain my little buddy, reminds me of her and how I want to live purposefully in her honor.

Thank you to Sebastian, who came into my life during the 4th quarter of this process and taught me that needles really can be found in haystacks.

Finally, thank you to B. In breaking my heart, you forced me to learn what I was made of, and as it turns out, it was better stuff than I thought.

About the Author

Unsure about entering the world, Tiffany Allen was forcibly removed from her warm, cozy hiding place with forceps.

Functioning in her role as oldest child further complicated the degree of comfort she felt in the world. Consequently, she's spent her life trying to live up to whatever she imagines is required. Presently a self-proclaimed "personal development" junkie, she's always on the hunt to unlock the key to her purpose and passion in life and laughing at herself along the way.

Tiffany lives in Seaside, CA where she ignores the bullet holes in her roof and prefers to spend her time relishing the blessing of waking up and looking out her kitchen window at the beautiful Monterey Bay. She spends her days as a Decision Support Analyst for a community hospital and her nights still trying to figure out what she wants to be when she grows up. Who knows? Maybe she'll be an author.

Thank you so much for your interest in my story and for putting your hard earned money toward the purchase of it. I am incredibly honored and grateful!

I have just one request.

Reviews are the lifeblood of a book.

I would be so appreciative if you would take a minute to give an honest review of _Carry On and Ditch the Excess Baggage!_ on Amazon.

Thank you again for your support!

Made in the USA
San Bernardino, CA
28 September 2016